# SURVIVAL

## Prepare Before
## Disaster STRIKES!

by

# Barbara Fix

**CCB Publishing**
**British Columbia, Canada**

Survival: Prepare Before Disaster Strikes

Copyright ©2011 by Barbara Fix
ISBN-13  978-1-927360-09-5
First Edition

Library and Archives Canada Cataloguing in Publication
Fix, Barbara, 1951-
Survival : prepare before disaster strikes / written by Barbara Fix.
Includes bibliographical references.
ISBN 978-1-927360-09-5
1. Emergency management--Handbooks, manuals, etc.
2. Preparedness--Handbooks, manuals, etc. I. Title.
HV551.2.F57 2011   613.6'9   C2011-907682-9

Cover art designed by: Juno Atkings.

Publisher:   CCB Publishing
British Columbia, Canada
www.ccbpublishing.com

## Dedication

This book is dedicated to the one-percenters who dig for the truth and prepare accordingly, and to my family members, who may not be used to a "backyard" that is shared with bears, coyotes, wolves and cougars, nonetheless come for visits over a campfire to enjoy the night sky…viewed best where city lights and pavement ends.

# Acknowledgements

I would like to thank Juno Atkings, graphic artist extraordinaire (who designed this book cover), self-taught editor and code de-coder, whose friendship and tireless help made this book possible. I would also like to thank Paul Rabinovitch, owner of CCB Publishing, who saw the need for *Survival: Prepare Before Disaster Strikes* to be in print and guided me through the process with the aplomb of a true professional.

# Contents

# Chapter 1

# Introduction

*"Man can live about forty days without food, about three days without water, about eight minutes without air, but only for one second without hope."*
Hal Lindsey

Preparedness has caught the attention of people from all walks of life: rich, poor and everyone in between. We all want the ability to be able to cook, eat and heat our homes during a disaster, whether an economic collapse, Mother Nature or a nuclear disaster has brought it on. *Survival: Prepare Before Disaster Strikes* is an easy to follow, economical guide to survival for those living in the city or the country.

At a time when the dollar has a nose bleed from its incredible dive into oblivion, when what we once took for granted has become a waiting game, seeking insurance against hunger is a reasonable goal. Many of us gambled on the equity of our homes and on jobs, but that gamble has crumbled like stale bread left too long in the sun. The crumbs we depended upon have been picked up and blown in the wind, carried to newly developing nations while on our soil we watch the division between rich and poor become greater than all other industrialized nations.

Never has there been more reason to prepare. It does not have to be done on a large scale, just small inroads, chinking away at that nagging feeling of unrest we are all feeling. Frugality, penny-pinching… call it what you will, but your journey should start with a squeeze-every-nickel budget.

When your pantries and basements begin to fill, your mood will lighten, and your feeling of helplessness will turn to resolve. Resolve

1

translates to strength, and with strength, you can change your future.

And don't think you can't do it. I did, a single woman, every bit in debt as most of the nation. I left my oversized home in the "burbs" and now homestead in North Idaho. Most of my family members see my resolve to prepare as unnecessary. But I continued to ignore them. I started by cutting the umbilical cord from a "shop 'till you drop" mentality. Now, many years later, I call a 900 sq. ft. cabin in the wilderness home. It has a well and a shed that holds enough food for twenty-two family members for one year; many of whom have placed bets on how long it will take for me to come to my senses… until the day when my resolve is needed. I plan to give them dish duty as penance.

I built this land-locked ark on research and determination, just as you can. Along the way, I made mistakes that I will share with you, so that your journey is made easier, and you in turn can make your own mistakes to share with others. I started with bags of rice and beans. I added to them, one sale at a time while researching that which common knowledge said could not be done; a way to preserve fresh eggs for months and cheese for years.

Today, waxed cheese hangs suspended from rustic rafters in my small kitchen. It's said it will last for years—some say up to 30—but that could be wildly optimistic. Recently, I taste-tested a slice of cheddar, then two years old, and it was delicious! In a crock sit eggs submerged in water glass that will last over winter.

When research warned yeast would be lifeless in 2 years after I'd already bought a boatload of it (Hey! We all suffer temporary setbacks), I looked for a workable solution. A trusted preparedness site promised sourdough was renewable as long as you fed and cared for it, just as you would any other living thing. But each recipe I found online said it must be refrigerated. Refrigeration was not part of my survival plan. How can the grid be trusted when it is vulnerable and run by bureaucrats? Days later, my laptop revealed that sourdough starter crossed over with Columbus in 1492. And it had hitchhiked in crocks against the chests of men brave enough to climb unfamiliar mountainsides during the Alaskan Gold Rush. There were no refrigerators in

Columbus' day and none on the backs of bearded men in the 1890's.

Refrigeration, I came to realize, was born of cushy lives. With that revelation came another. I had lost the ability to think for myself. Like many of us, I had grown complacent with my cushy life and had lost the ability to survive. If you doubt this, just think back to Hurricane Katrina.

Our forefathers knew how to survive. I suspect their DNA was "set" to intuit survival much like a newborn calf knows to head for the udder without invitation. But somehow, over the ensuing decades there was a disconnect. For answers, we depend on the "experts" to tell us how to live. Unfortunately their advice is dependant upon grocers, the electrical grid, municipal water, and natural gas to bath, heat our homes, provide light, and to cook.

But there is hope. By the time you've finished reading this book, you will have an understanding of sustainable preparedness; how to survive if the plug is pulled on the grid and municipal water, how and what to store for survival, and why the smartest gardeners buy heirloom seed. The bravest of you might graduate to raising chickens and goats, and should you choose to, you'll be able to preserve farm-fresh eggs and cheese and keep sourdough starter on the counter without it escaping its crock; possibly laying claim to the kitchen and part of the living room.

My personal exodus from the city landed intentionally away from potential looters with a well that is a far cry safer and accessible than city water. I remain financially challenged, just as you may be on your journey into self-sufficiency. But better to have a basement full of life-sustaining food, and a woodstove to warm you, than a room full of gold or designer clothes vainly collecting dust.

I'm convinced I will never be finished with my preparations. I doubt that you will be either. There is always a goal just out of reach. Mine is an ATV. It would be nice to have a mode of transportation when calamity strikes.

In the meantime, many years of research made the impossible

3

possible while I learned there are many ways to stretch a dollar, even a dollar as disastrously devalued as ours. There are free blogs offering food storage recipes, farmers who will happily sell you beans, wheat, fruits, and vegetables for pennies on the dollar, random grocery stores not so greedy they won't sell you bulk goods at a fair price (bless them), craigslist for cheap supplies, and survival and preparedness websites whose generous wisdom will share how you can avoid standing in line for a handout when calamity strikes.

You may have to abandon your TV… hit the off switch, for there isn't time to laze around. But there is the Internet and used bookstores and libraries, where you can devour the information that will further enlighten you on the skills you will need to survive.

This journey does not include vacations to sandy beaches, or $200 designer jeans and nights out on the town. Those are frivolous things, at best, when pitted against the ability to eat. I hope that you are blessed in this journey, that others will take up the baton and save you isolation. But if not, press forward anyway. Along the way, once some of your preparations are done, when you send off for heirloom seed whose yield will not shrivel to the earth or poison you, and you have a moments respite, give yourself a pat on the back for a job well done.

# Chapter 2

# Are You Ready?

*"Every survival kit should include a sense of humor."*
Author unknown.

It's 1:45 on a Tuesday afternoon. The office is quiet and your thoughts travel to what to make for dinner tonight. As you jot down a grocery list, the radio station you are listening to is interrupted with an attention signal from the Emergency Broadcast System. You tune out the irritating blare. They've been stepping up the tests to the point that it serves only as a mild disruption, nothing more. Your list is complete. As you lay down the pen, it occurs to you the voice coming from the radio is not the same recorded voice you've grown used to with other broadcasts. You turn up the volume on the radio and suddenly your blood runs cold "…nuclear attack," the announcer says. Where? You listen, holding your breath as your heart races. "You are advised to remain indoors until further notice. Please stay tuned to the emergency broadcast system for further instructions. I repeat, this is the National…"

You are up and out of your seat. You grab your purse from the top of your desk and sprint down the hallway. Co-workers are milling about, their faces registering shock and disbelief. But there isn't time to join them and try to make sense of the broadcast. You have one question, and you ask it of your boss as he exits the conference room. "Where was the attack?"

He continues walking towards the clutch of employees crowding near the receptionist's desk, his expression unreadable. "Las Vegas. A suitcase bomb!" he replies, continuing his determined stride to the biggest concentration of employees, possibly to calm them, or to advise them, but you will never know because your goal is to make it to your son's school before the roads are hopelessly gridlocked.

The elevators have gone to other floors and several crowding the bank of elevator's are staring nervously at the uncooperative steel doors. You turn and follow the hallway to the stairwell and start down the stairs at a jog. The parking lot is seven stories down and the stairs are a blur as you take inventory of the situation. Las Vegas is 1,100 miles from Seattle. Your family has dogged the first bullet, but your getaway cabin is on Whidbey Island. Will the ferry be running? If it is, it runs to Whidbey every half-hour, so no time constraints there. But first, you will need to make the 35-mile drive to the Mukilteo Ferry. If luck isn't with you, and the terminal is deserted when you arrive, you will need to make the 100-mile drive, some of it on narrow, secondary roads. Impossible! The roads will be choked with evacuees before you even reach your son's school. Best to head home, and sort it out from there…

Your mind grasps for something positive to hold on to, something that holds more answers than questions and lands on the contents of your trunk; three overstuffed emergency backpacks and a couple of duffle bags filled with cooking supplies and camping gear. Your sigh of relief comes out in a huff of overworked lungs. And boots! Just last week you stuffed new hiking boots for everyone in the last available corner of the trunk. Even if the ferry isn't running and it turns out your family will have to wait out the first wave of the backlash at home, your have MRE's and water stored in the basement that will see you through. Your townhouse is nine miles away. If need be, you and your son will walk home, you tell yourself, as your pumps cut into the tops of your feet.

The parking lot is surprisingly full, nearly as full as this morning when you'd parked. A handful of people are walking to their cars and you recognize several co-workers. No one says a word. In fact, there is no noise at all. Even the birds are silent. Your peripheral vision catches the flash of metal moving towards you, and you dodge out of the way.

The driver continues to tear out of the parking lot without glancing in your direction. They don't get far. Cars on the arterial in front of the building aren't moving and you are confronted with the first hurdle bridging the distance between you and your ten-year-old son.

Backing your car out of its spot, you head down the alleyway that spills onto a back street, away from the congestion. The neighborhood you travel is made up of desperately stacked 60's-era apartments. The afternoon breeze carries through open windows into cramped living spaces as cooking smells waft through the air.

Residents are congregated here and there, gesturing in panic as if the coming devastation will go away so long as they stand near cars or on front lawns and voice their fears. You're forced to navigate around hastily opened car doors on the narrow roadway as residents dump household goods and electronics into the backseats and trunks of their cars. They resemble busy ants whose nest has been disturbed; up worn stairs and back down to deposit more useless junk and it suddenly occurs to you most of these people will be a statistic if things get bad. How were TV's, computers and Nintendo's going to feed and shelter them? They wouldn't!

You force yourself to tune out your thoughts: There is nothing you can do to change the outcome, not when your worst imaginings are being announced on the radio and you are still miles away from your son's school.

It's slow going, but the traffic is creeping forward a little at a time. You turn up the radio and a public service announcer is spilling out information, barely coming up for air. "Initial reports are the blast went off on the Las Vegas Strip. At this time the number of casualties has not been determined. You are advised to remain in your homes..." You turn off your radio, unable to hear more. Not until you've picked up your son. Your husband is clear across town—downtown, to be exact.

Pulling your cell phone from your purse, you scroll through the contact list to your son's school and hit send. You never got around to asking the school what their emergency policy was. What if they are on lockdown? It might be…how can they put students on a bus when some would be arriving to empty homes while their parents are stuck in gridlock? Hopefully, someone would be manning the doors and allow you to enter to claim your son.

The cell phone gives you a fast busy signal and a tentacle of fear wraps around you like a cold shroud. You try again. This time the call is placed to your husband. He could have been away from the office and somehow beaten the worst of the traffic. With luck, he could be at the school now. You hit send and get another fast busy signal. It's no good. The traffic slows to a stop. Horns blare and the cars ahead of you take to the shoulder of the road to go around a stalled car. They must have run out of gas, you decide. Every gas station you've passed had impossible lines of drivers waiting their turn at the pumps. You follow the drivers ahead of you and move to the shoulder to get around an old station wagon, your thoughts alternating between worry over whether you will be allowed inside the school, and relief that your basement shelves are ready for whatever lies ahead.

It takes 45 minutes to drive the seven miles to your son's school and during that time you've attempted to reach the school and your husband dozens of times with no results. The parking lot is full, forcing you to snag a parking spot on the street. You frantically search for your husband's car, but it isn't there. The next few minutes rest upon a policy maker with the school district, you realize, as your hurried steps approach the front steps of the school.

\* \* \* \* \*

The above scenario is but one in a long list of possibilities. A crisis could just as easily be the result of an earthquake, or a banking crash, throwing the already belabored nation into panic. No matter what the crisis, the extent of preparations and planning you invest in survival now will have a direct bearing on how drastic the impact of a crisis is on you and your loved ones.

## Hit the Ground Running

Being as physically fit as possible will increase your chances of surviving a crisis. Assess your physical condition honestly. Do you believe you are capable of walking miles to safety if you had to, or would you cower for cover? If the answer is the latter, you can start making small improvements by walking a few blocks each day and increase your distance a little at a time. If your days are crammed with work and taking care of others once you arrive home, you might consider committing half of your lunch hour to walking. Keeping a stationary bicycle at home (but not using it as a clothes hanger!) or joining a gym are other possibilities. Perhaps swimming interests you. It doesn't take a Herculean effort to gain back what may have been lost over the years and you might even discover you like the new you! You shouldn't be expected to suffer alone with this, so snag a friend or a family member to join you—play the guilt card if that's what it takes.

Your goal is simply to condition your body to accept the rigors of walking long distances. When your muscles are acclimated to physical activity, you will be less likely to seize up when placing sudden demands on your body.

If you have physical limitations that would make walking or hiking difficult or impossible, this should be discussed with family members or those in your group, so alternative arrangements can be made to get you to safety.

## Back to School

If you've never taken a CPR or first aid course, or enough time has lapsed that you have forgotten most of what you learned, it's time to sign up for class. During a crisis, outside help may not be available for hours or days, so it is important to understand the basics. You will need a detailed, easy to follow book on first aid. Jot one down at the top of your preparedness list.

Take a self-defense class. No one wants to think about having to defend themselves at a time when we should be helping one another, but the truth is there will be opportunists willing to do whatever it takes to survive. If you encounter such a person, being able to disarm them will allow you to flee to safety. If you are on a tight budget, check with your local YMCA as many locations offer inexpensive self-defense classes.

## 72-Hour Emergency Kit Accessibility

There is no way to know the exact day or hour when a crisis may strike. The best you can do is access and prepare for any dangers your location is likely to experience, especially with regards to earthquakes, mudslides, hurricanes, and flash floods. Ask your city planners what contingencies they have in place for emergencies and find out where your area shelters are located in the event of nuclear attack (more on this later in the chapter).

For the most part, preparedness will cover most contingencies. Even so, your personal safety could be directly tied to getting where you need to be. This is made much easier with a 72-hour emergency kit that contains three days worth of basic survival goods. Recommended items are listed at the end of this chapter. These kits are sometimes referred to as emergency kits, 72-hour kits, bug-out kits, or grab-and-go kits, but whatever one chooses to call them, there are an alarming number of folks who recommend they be stored at home. I have a short, concise retort for that notion: Dumb idea! If you are at work or out running errands when a disaster strikes, the roads will quickly become gridlocked, especially if you live in the city, while your emergency kit is stored uselessly in your basement. I rest my case.

Emergency kits are meant to provide food, emergency shelter, communications (wind-up or battery-run radio) and basic medical supplies to get you past the initial confusion and gridlock that comes with a disaster. They are nothing less than a lifeline that will see you through a disaster until you're able to make it home or to your getaway location safely. If you take prescription medicine, it is important to have extra medicine tucked away in your emergency kit. For those of you who commute or carpool to work, it is wise to keep an extra emergency kit at work.

## Time for an Escape Plan

As reflected in the scenario presented at the beginning of this chapter, it is important to find out what the emergency plan for your child's school is, or if applicable, their daycare. Will your child be evacuated to another location in the event of a weather related disaster, or an earthquake, or a terrorist attack? If so, find out where that location is. Ask if you will be allowed to pick up your child and if you can appoint a designated contact person to pick them up in the event you are unable to reach them yourself. If so, be sure to give the school or daycare their name and give your signed consent to your contact person.

Select an alternate designated contact person who lives outside your immediate area who is unlikely to have experienced the same emergency as your location. If for any reason you become separated from a member of your family or group, and landline and cellular service is **operable**, the designated person can relay messages to help calm any fears over the safety of those missing.

Having just discussed designating a phone contact, it is important that you do not rely on your cell phone's storage capabilities to access emergency contact numbers (more on this later on in the chapter under *When Communications Fail*). Here's where nagging is perfectly acceptable. Make sure everyone has the designated person's phone number written down and available at all times. Unfortunately, procrastination is a fact of life for many of us, but procrastination does not get along well with a crisis.

If your area takes a direct hit in a disaster, it is possible your neighborhood will be under evacuation orders. If this occurs, police and military personnel will be evacuating people *out* of the area and you may find yourself unable to get past roadblocks. Most of us have watched newscasts of residents forced out of their homes during a wildfire. And we've seen those same residents arguing with authorities to let them return. To my knowledge, none of them came out the victor. This situation highlights why you must have an emergency kit available for each member of your family or group.

You should select an alternative meeting place, away from home, in the case of evacuation. Each member must be familiar with the chosen location and a dry run, much like a fire drill, should be practiced. If things go wrong during the exercise, you'll have plenty of time for re-do's.

## Familiarize Yourself with Breakers & Shut-Offs

If you're woken in the middle of the night to mayhem; grab a flashlight (always keep one at your bedside) to make a home inspection. If you have natural gas lines running into your home, **never** flip on a light switch or use a candle or a lighter to inspect your home. This can be the vector to ignite built-up gas fumes.

Here's an example: in the 80's, two men from the gas company were sent to inspect a gas leak in a derelict building. Most of the bare light bulbs in the hallway of the building had been broken out; so one of the men flicked his Bic lighter. The result made him a candidate for the Darwin Awards.

Natural gas has an odorant added to it so it is easily detected. Natural gas must have the right concentration of fumes for it to be life threatening, but don't risk it! If you detect a gas leak, get everyone outdoors, pronto, and keep the door open on the way out to let the dangerous fumes escape.

If you have propane appliances or a heating system, it is important to understand that unlike natural gas, propane is heavier than air, and does not dissipate into the air as readily as does natural gas. The same rules apply for a propane leak as they do with natural gas—get everyone outdoors, leaving the door open. Propane will settle to the lower levels of your home such as the floor, a basement, or crawl space and it will take longer to clear out of living spaces.

Familiarize yourself with the location of your natural gas or propane shut-off, and in the event of a leak, turn it off immediately. Propane will have a service valve on the tank, whereas natural gas shut-off valves are located on the meter, which is typically installed outside against the foundation of the house, but this can vary. In the event of a leak, turn the valve to the off position.

Some emergencies require turning off the power to your home at the electrical panel. Circuit breakers are typically behind an easily identifiable panel. Every member of the family old enough to be of help in a crisis should be taught about utility shut-offs to your home.

Water main shut-offs aren't always as easy to find, especially in older homes where they can be buried in an obscure corner of a basement or crawlspace. I speak from experience. Having just finished renovations on a Victorian home, I was showing off the years of hard work to my brother and sister-in-law. Suddenly the wall in the entryway began to spout water (reminding me about the consequences of pride). It looked as if someone had turned on a showerhead at full force as water gushed down the stairway and onto the foyer. My brother ran to the netherworlds of the 1890-era basement to look for the water shut-off with the spiders and the other creepy-crawlies, and my sister-in-law and I began frantically sweeping the worst of the flood out the front door and onto the frozen veranda.

Ten minutes later, the torrent had only grown stronger as it blew out the newly installed drywall and I ran for the phone to call the fire department—hey, plumbers can take hours to reach—when we heard a muffled voice calling triumphantly from below; "Found it!"

It turned out the water shut-off was hidden in a crawlspace, tucked away from the finished basement where a century's worth of old doors and trim lay. My advice is to take the time to find out where your water shut-off is located now, before an emergency, so you won't be floundering in the dark wondering if you'll ever find it.

## When You Are the Fireman

You should purchase several ABC fire extinguishers for emergencies. Why specifically an ABC model? They use monoammonium phosphate, designed to put out liquid fires, combustible material fires, as well as electrical fires. So cover your bets with an all-inclusive extinguisher.

Remember, your local fire department may not be able to reach you in the case of fire or other emergencies during a full-blown crisis. Landline and cell phone coverage may be down or jammed. With the use of candles, oil lamps, and cooking with an unfamiliar heat source during a power outage, the possibility of fire increases.

If your home has a fire-burning devise such as a woodstove or fireplace you will need chimney fire retardant in case of a chimney fire. If the chimney flu hasn't been cleaned recently, it should be checked for creosote buildup. Make sure your wood heat stove or wood cook stove has a protective, non-flammable barrier installed behind and under them such as cement board, sheet metal, or ceramic tile.

## Keep Your Car Emergency Ready

It is important to keep your gas tank as full as possible for reliable transportation in the event of a crisis. Gas pumps may be inoperable due to power outages, and even when the grid is working, the pumps will soon run out of gasoline. Any auto repairs that have been put off should be addressed as soon as possible. Be sure you have a dependable spare tire and keep a can of Fix-A-Flat or something similar on hand. The donut tires supplied with newer cars are not meant for long drives, and they certainly aren't designed for the off-road driving you may find yourself having to perform when navigating around stalled cars. Keep extra motor oil, jumper cables, a jack, lug wrench, a basic toolkit, and a battery-run air pump stored in your car. You'll find a suggested list at the end of this chapter

Keep important documentation accessible: Birth certificates, last will and testament, health insurance documentation, health records, inoculation records, marriage certificate, driver's license, Social Security documentation, school records, Tax (IRS) paperwork, automobile title, mortgage information, automobile and homeowner's insurance documentation (proving your policy is current), property tax information, banking and all other financial documentation such as annuities, 401K and other retirement plans, and stocks and bonds.

This is only the most basic of paperwork you will need. From there, you will want to build your own list dependent upon your specific circumstances. Keeping copies of these documents in your car, or the office if you commute to work, is the obvious solution. If you are worried about sensitive information getting into the wrong hands, consider blacking out account numbers with an indelible marking pen and jotting them down on a separate piece of paper that can be tucked away in your wallet. To be doubly certain, you might consider keeping duplicate copies at home, at your workplace, and your getaway destination, if applicable.

Unfortunately, emergencies do not come gift wrapped with instructions before hand, but it's possible the Internet may experience disruptions. Institutions depend almost exclusively on digitized bytes for their records and you will need proof of your banking information, or that you hold title to your car or home, and you will want to be able to prove insurance coverage on your car and home. Short of that, you may find yourself in enough red tape to ticker tape the next Macy's Day Parade!

## Beat the Bank Crunch

Depending upon the emergency, it is possible banks will be closed for an extended period of time. During such an event, having as much cash on hand as possible will be a saving grace. Services such as grocers and hardware stores may still be open and you may need cash to purchase the goods and services you need. Keep small denominations—no more than $1's, $5's, and $10's in case change for purchases is unavailable. I realize many have invested in gold, which has sky-rocketed as the dollar continues its nosedive. But to have only bullion to offer in exchange for something like a loaf of bread when there is no change would be a terrible situation to be in. If you prefer tangible currency that will hold its value, consider keeping at least part of your investments in silver coins. That way the loss, should change be unavailable, will be merely an annoyance.

The amount of cash you will want to have on hand varies with each person's circumstances. Will you be driving a long distance to a getaway destination? If so, you will need cash for things like tires, snow chains, and sundry goods. But whatever you do, be sure to calculate your gas needs and have that available and stored in a safe place in transportable gas cans. It is almost a certainty that you will not find available gas during an extended trip.

## When Communications Fail

When preparing for an emergency, it is wise to make contingency plans in the event communications are down, if only for a short time. EMP pulse from the sun or weaponry can render communication systems inoperable. Telco buildings are not known for overabundant security to protect them. Telecommunications are dependent on the electrical grid and battery backup, satellite, microwave, T-1 lines, and in the case of some cellular providers, are reliant on landline phone companies for switching services to hand off phone calls for their customers. Additionally, it is a common occurrence for landline and cell phone lines to get jammed during an emergency. Because of this, it isn't prudent to expect your cell or landline phone to be operable during a national or local emergency. So please do not put all your eggs in that basket!

## Sheltering in Place

Even when plans are to relocate to an alternate location, you should put aside food, water, and medical supplies, and have a workable solution for cooking and heating at home. If roads are gridlocked or blockaded due to dangerous conditions, travel may be impossible at the onset of a crisis. In the case of climatic disaster, roadways may remain impassable. To have all your preparedness goods in one location, outside walking distance to your home, leaves room for failure and failure in a time of crisis is *not* an option.

## Use What You Have Wisely

If the electrical grid goes down in your area, stretch your food storage by consuming what is in the refrigerator first (with the exception of freezer perishables like ice cream). Consume frozen goods next, making certain to open the refrigerator and freezer as little as possible to avoid warming the interior.

## Nature's Meal Plan

I highly recommend including a book on edible plants with your emergency kit. Most likely, it will never be needed. For such a book to be a necessary, the state of the emergency would have to be of gargantuan proportions; either that, or you finally found the time and money for that dream vacation and Murphy's Law took a chokehold on your plans. Still, it may be the best $10 you will ever spend if you find yourself stranded. Many books written on edible plants and herbs are zone specific, and if you can locate one for your climate zone, I suggest you buy it. I purchased two such books. My favorite, *Edible Wild Plants: A North American Field Guide* by Elias & Dykeman, gives a close-up color photograph of the plant or herb. When a poisonous look-alike exists, the reader is warned and is supplied with a detailed description and a photograph of the imposter. It also supplies a state map next to the plant's photograph, highlighting the area(s) where it grows and a description of where it is likely to be located (example: in moist fertile soil, at the margins of woods, etc...). It advises what time of year to harvest the plant or herb, how to cook it, and its nutritional benefits.

## Stake Your Water Claim

Chapter 3 is devoted to water sources, purification, and storage, but as water is imperative for survival, we will touch upon it here. In a preparedness plan, water must always come first, for without it, you might as well use this and any other preparedness book you may read for kindling. Begin your preparedness with stored water and a good quality water purifier such as a Berkey or Katadyn. If the grid goes down and you live in an area that depends on municipal water supplies, you may continue to receive water, but only as long as the water plant's battery or diesel backup lasts.

If the electrical grid goes down during a crisis, this is an excellent time to fill bathtubs and sinks with every drop of water they will hold. But be careful. When calamity arrives in the form of Mother Nature, it is possible the water pouring from your taps may be unsafe to drink. Listen to emergency broadcasts on your hand-crank or battery-run radio (Yes, you do need one!) for alerts on water contamination.

## Vanity Makes House Calls

For all my years of preparedness, I've cast my net far and stood toe to toe with trading a once spoiled consumer-crazed lifestyle for that of a penny-pincher in order to fill empty storage shelves. But even then, I can't conceive of a time when bathing, or doing laundry, or washing dishes would be considered a luxury.

The fault, I've decided, lies with Hollywood. Do you recall even a B-movie of apocalyptic proportions panning in on an actor whose hair has turned to dreadlocks, wearing filthy clothing with dirt embedded under their nails? Well, neither do I!

But the reality is, if we don't plan ahead, that's where we'll find ourselves. Arrange for a makeshift tub for bathing because unless you have a well with a manual hand pump and a septic system, once the battery backup gives out at the municipal water station, it's likely your tub and sinks won't drain when pumps become inoperable in a grid-down situation. Tuff Stuff makes tubs that work well for bathing that are relatively cheap. While you're purchasing the tub, pick up a clothesline and clothes pegs. At the end of this chapter, I have listed the link for a do-it-yourself washing machine made out of a 5-gallon bucket and a toilet plunger. No, I'm not kidding!

## It's a Stinky Subject

At a time when water and electricity has been knocked off grid, waste management will have to be addressed. Compost toilets are available that can be neutralized with sawdust or dirt, but if you live in the city with little if any yard, I can't see a landlord agreeing to let you store a mound of either material. The best option for those living in an urban setting is a camp toilet. There's nothing "bling" about them, but at least they come with a toilet seat and a collapsible lid, and they cost next to nothing. Line them with heavy plastic bags so the contents can be carefully transferred outdoors. If possible, dig a hole deep enough for sanitary disposal.

In rural areas, an outhouse will solve the problem of waste issues, no matter how long a crisis lasts. For those of you who live in the suburbs, I don't see how CCR'S will preclude an outhouse when the alternative leads to disease and health risks. If you have any doubts, an outhouse that resembles a shed will work—the "don't ask, don't tell" dictum can have you breathing easy through a difficult time. I doubt you will be breaking any rules by using it once things have gone south.

It might take children time to get used to these new accommodations, so even if you have the Cadillac of outhouses, think about keeping a camp toilet or a port-a-potty on hand for in-home use. If an outhouse is in your future *after* the fact, make sure you have a heavy-duty shovel and enough plywood, 2X4's, roofing material, nails and screws to build one. The end of this chapter lists a link for an excellent site that has do-it-yourself instructions on building an outhouse.


## Where To?

You should store both topographical and street maps in your vehicle that covers your immediate location and on to your destination point, no matter how many maps this may entail. Keep a compass in your car to navigate to your destination. Even in a worst case scenario, and you must walk part of the way to your destination, you will have the means to get there (and the reason for keeping topographical maps).

Never depend on GPS or any other digital navigational device that depends upon electricity to relay or download your coordinates. Why? Your device may be battery-run, and you may have thought ahead and put extra batteries aside, but should your GPS provider depend on electricity (and they do), with grid failure comes eventual GPS failure. GPS devices have another issue that involves terrain that is referred to as line of site. Line of site simply means data is grabbed from your GPS device and downloaded to you via a straight line from an orbiting satellite or a relay site to you, the user. Line of site does not move around corners or "dip" down between mountain ranges when you happen to be in a deep valley surrounded by a mountain range. They are also a bit temperamental about traveling through a solid mass such as a tall building. A bit of trivia: this is why your cell phone coverage is sometimes disrupted when traveling in valley or mountainous regions. Never trade a compass for GPS.


## When It's Time to Leave

The emergency kits stored in your car may not be needed solely at the start of a crisis, and if this is the case, you will want to transfer your items from your car to your home or getaway location, behind closed doors for safekeeping. The first reaction to a crisis may freeze people into inactivity, but if the emergency is prolonged, and people begin to run out of food and water, looting *will* follow. It may be that your location is safe at first, but as time goes on, and looting increases, it may become necessary to get away from your present location and flee to a safer place. In most cases, this is likely to be to a wooded area.

Take a few practice runs to the area of your choice and camp overnight. If camping isn't allowed at your "safe place", then use an alternate for practice. Test your skills with building a campfire, putting up a tent, and cooking meals over an open fire or a camp stove. If you've never been camping, now is the time to learn! But remember: bring comfortable, layered clothing and hiking boots or high-topped tennis shoes. A reference guide like the Boy Scout Manual will see you through. It has solid information on camping, building a campfire and camp-style cooking.

Practice using your water purifier, and eating the MRE's or canned goods you've put aside for a crisis. That way, you will be better prepared both emotionally and logistically for a smooth transition when disaster strikes.

Keep mental notes on your progress. If you discover you forgot a bowl to mix the pancake batter in, throw it in with your emergency supplies once you return home. That same bowl can be used to scoop water from a creek or a lake to pour through a water purifier. If the bowl happens to be metal, it can be used to cook with if need be. If you forget matches or a hatchet or newspaper and find yourself unable to start a campfire to keep warm by, this is the reason why you've taken this weekend getaway. Developing camping skills takes practice. There is nothing more eye opening than spending a night shivering in the cold to be reminded of the need to prepare.

**Survival Note:** Keep all foods and garbage stored **away** from your campsite area, as food smells will attract animals—some more dangerous than others.

## Alternative Modes of Transportation

Brainstorm alternative modes of transportation for a time when you may have to relocate. A mountain bike, dirt bike, ATV 4-wheeler, or a motorcycle will help get you safely to your chosen destination when roads are not navigable. If your mode of transportation is motorized, set aside gasoline containing fuel additives to extend its life in a portable gas container with a pour spout. It must be stored in a safe place, away from the home and open flame sources like that of a heater or hot water heater.

## Traveling During or Directly After a Crisis

If you must travel during or directly after a crisis, be especially careful of downed power lines. In the case of an earthquake or flood, be cautious when crossing a bridge, as the foundation may have been weakened with the movement of the earth. Watch for roads that may be crumbling or otherwise weakened.

## There's Safety in Numbers

If you live alone, consider banning together with others. During a crisis, isolation will leave you more vulnerable to looters and opportunists. Physiologically, it is better to be with others you can talk to and lean on as you help one another through the stressful times that lay ahead. Why not open up the subject with neighbors, friends, or family members?

## Surviving a Nuclear Attack

There are ways to protect yourself in the event of nuclear attack. Ingesting iodine or iodine tablets can help control the damage of radioactive exposure, specifically thyroid cancer that can result at a later date after exposure. Pregnant and nursing women and those with small children should seek medical advice before ingesting iodine. An allergy to iodine is rare, but if you are prone to allergies, and especially if you have had a reaction to shell fish (they contain iodine), it is best to get tested before ingesting iodine. Signs of allergic reaction are nausea, flushing, fever, or labored breathing. Seek medical help if this occurs.

Suggested doses are 16mg for infants; 32 mg for children, and 50 to 70 mg for adults. Dosages must be taken for 14 consecutive days.

K-1 was given to children during the Chernobyl nuclear meltdown with positive results. Potassium iodide works by "saturating" the thyroid with stable iodide so it's less likely to absorb radioactive iodine that is released during a nuclear event. Under current dosing guidelines, a fully saturated thyroid would be protected for up to one month, which is typically long enough for radioactive iodine (which has a half life of 8 days) to dissipate from the environment. The exception to this is an event like the Fukushima nuclear meltdown that continues to carry radiation via trade winds on a global scale.

Either potassium iodide (K-103), or potassium iodide (K-1) will work, but you will need slightly more K-103 than K-1.

Wearing a simple cloth facemask found at drug and hardware stores will help reduce exposure to radioactive fallout. You cannot see, smell, or taste fallout, so do not be deceived into thinking your surroundings are safe and follow the information you are given over emergency broadcasts. It is imperative to stay indoors during a nuclear attack.

If you are traveling and get notification from the Emergency Radio Broadcast System or a local news station of a nuclear attack, drive immediately to the nearest shelter if possible. Most shelters are designed for fallout protection. Be sure to familiarize yourself with the location of fallout shelters in your area.

If you are traveling and are unable to reach a fallout shelter, seek a culvert or a location where you are protected from the out of doors and sheltered by earth, as it will help absorb some of the radiation. The effect of fallout is cumulative, therefore, long exposure to radiation, or continued on and off exposure can build up in the body which can lead to health risks.

If you are at the office or at home when a nuclear attack occurs, you should move to a basement if possible. Remember, being below ground level will protect you from the worst of the fallout. Never go outdoors until you are given notice it is safe to do so.

Should a basement be unavailable, stay to the center of the building, as far away from window and door openings as possible. If there is time and you have the materials on hand, cover doorways and windows with heavy-mill plastic sheeting and secure it with duct tape.

When the immediate danger has passed, and if you suspect you were exposed to radioactive fallout, strip off all clothing and place them in a bag, which should be stored away from your immediate area. Wash your hair and skin thoroughly with water, but do not scrub, as this could rub fallout particles into your skin.

*The following is a breakdown of various locations and their degrees of exposure to fallout:*

Outdoors – Very little Protection
Home or Office – Medium Protection
Basement – Better Protection
Fallout Shelter – Optimal Protection

Root cellars can serve as a fallout shelter when built properly. Shelters can be constructed in basements or can be dug in-ground or into a hillside. To get the most protection against fallout, incorporate any one of the methods listed below:

16 inches of solid brick
16 inches of hollow concrete blocks filled with mortar or sand
2 feet of packed earth, or 3 feet if loose earth
5 inches of steel
3 inches of lead
3 feet of water

There is no way to predict the exact impact of a nuclear attack without the advice of experts trained to measure fallout and its trajectory. The spread of fallout is dependent upon a bomb's yield, and whether impact was at ground level or if it was detonated above ground. An above ground explosion will spread radioactive fallout further (as experienced with Fukushima).

Another factor considered when predicting radioactive fallout is wind; the direction it is traveling, and the velocity of the prevailing winds that carry the plume. It is possible that radioactive fallout may be spread for hundreds or thousands of miles and may have long-lasting health effects for anyone exposed. Conversely, the majority of damage from a nuclear blast might be contained within a 15-mile radius.

Rain or snowfall will spread fallout. Radioactive particles in the atmosphere are collected in precipitation and are carried to the ground, creating "hot spots".

If you receive news of an imminent nuclear attack and you are **certain** there is a space of time before impact, gather whatever food or preparedness goods that you will need from outdoor storage (including your vehicle) and move them to the lowest spot in your home— preferably a basement or to the center of the space you will be occupying.

Be sure to include a battery-run or a wind-up emergency radio with your provisions. A radio will be your lifeline over the next few weeks after a nuclear event, letting you know the circumstances and impact of a nuclear event. Be sure to include clothing, medicine (including prescription medicine), bedding or sleeping bags, and a camp toilet. Keep several flashlights and extra batteries on hand where you will be sheltering, as it is possible that the electrical grid may go down.

**It is important** to store at least two weeks worth of water and food for your family or group indoors, *before* an emergency strikes. To go in search of water or food items stored in a shed or outbuilding after a nuclear event will expose you to fallout, and should concentrations be heavy enough, exposure can lead to death.

You should keep all pets indoors, and don't forget to grab their food if it's stored outdoors or in an outbuilding.

As already mentioned, heavy-mill plastic sheeting can be fitted to windows and doorways with duct tape to better protect indoor spaces. Turn off air conditioning and heating systems that draw outside air into your home.

Try to remain calm. Busy work in times of stress can help take your mind off the uncertainty of the next few minutes or hours. Keep your radio tuned to information that will keep you abreast of the situation and help you plan for what lays ahead.

After a nuclear blast, remain indoors. Canned, boxed, or food stored in buckets that have not been left open to be exposed to the elements (radiation), can be eaten. But first, they must be wiped down before opening. Be sure to keep your hands and the area under your fingernails clean to avoid transferring fallout material to the food. Fruits that have an outer protection such as a banana or an orange can be wiped clean and carefully peeled before consuming. Any foods that are left exposed, such as a canister of flour or sugar that does not have a protective lid should not be consumed as ingesting contaminated food may lead to internal damage.

Water stored in containers is safe to drink as long as it was kept covered. In most cases, water drawn from a covered well is also safe to drink and cook with. However, if you suspect your well water may have been contaminated, follow the *Fallout Filtering Methods* found in Chapter 3.

If you rely on city water, once stored water has run out, listen to your local radio station for information on the advisability of drinking or cooking with your area's water supply.

If the only water source available is from a lake, stream, or pond, you must filter water before drinking or cooking with it after a nuclear event. A water purifier **will not** remove fallout. See instructions in Chapter 3 under *Fallout Filtering Methods* for instructions on purifying contaminated water.

If radioactive particles have come into contact with your skin, you may experience burns within a few hours. Radiation illness will not spread to others except for nausea soon after being exposed. Serious signs of radiation illness are as follows: hair loss, loss of appetite, paleness, diarrhea, sore throat, bleeding gums, and easy bruising. If you or anyone in your group experiences any of these ailments, you should seek medical attention.

## Emergency Kits, Automobile Safety & Camping Gear

The following are items you should have available for emergency kits, automobile safety, and camping gear preparedness. The recommended foods are intentionally simple, meant for easy preparation. Keep in mind: if you are caught far away from home, or worse, stranded for any length of time, you will wonder why you hadn't thought to include many of the items mentioned below.

**72-Hour Emergency Kit:** Battery-run, wind-up, or solar powered radio, water purifier, canteen/water bottles, magnesium flint and steel fire starter, matches, MRE's, baby food, formula and diapers (if applicable), water, knife, flashlight (include a shaker style for when batteries run out), batteries, wire, two-way radios, nylon rope, prescription medicine, medical supplies, duct tape, first aid book, edible plants and herbs book and important documents.

**Camping Gear:** Tent, duffle bags for each person, sleeping bags for each person—rated for your climate zone, warm blankets, Swiss-style army knife, fishing pole and fishing tackle, weapon and ammunition, rope/twine, clothes pens, battery-run or propane lantern, lantern fuel or extra batteries, lantern socks, tarp, camp stove, camp stove fuel, hatchet, axe, tree limbing saw, newspaper (to start fires) and waterproof matches.

**First Aid:** First aid book (also listed under 72-hour emergency kit section), rubbing alcohol, hydrogen peroxide, antacid, anti-diarrhea medicine, thermometer, aspirin, children's pain medication, bandages, gauze, gauze pads, surgical tape, suture pack, ace bandage, calamine lotion, daily prescription medicines, antibiotic ointment, eye wash and ointment, contact lens wash, anti-fungal ointment, pain and anti-inflammatory medication, burn treatment ointment or spray, iodine, electrolyte drinks (for dehydration), cold remedies—children and adult, cough medicine, cough drops, scissors, tweezers and needles (for splinter removal), sun block, mosquito spray, dental kit for denture repair, and toothache gels.

**Cooking Supplies** can be stored in a cooler for portability. You will need: fire pit grate, (camp stove—already listed under camping gear section), cooking spices, cooking oil, Dutch oven, frying pan and pots (best if they're cast iron), unbreakable dishes, eating utensils, camp-style coffee maker, mixing bowls (metal can be used to cook with), spatula, stir spoon, metal drinking cups, can openers, dish soap, dish towel, matches or lighters—there's NO such thing as too many matches, scrubbing pads, buckets, zip-lock bags, tin foil, plastic wrap, hot pads and canned goods.

**Clothing:** Hiking boots/high top tennis shoes, socks, stocking cap, gloves, jacket, bandana, extra changes of clothes and underwear—always plan ahead for clothing appropriate to your climate zone and don't count on warm weather if your area has distinct seasons. Many of us have been caught in a freak snowfall, especially in mountainous areas. Never assume that summertime means packing shorts and T-shirts!

**Hygiene Products:** Shampoo, body soap, solar camp shower, hand lotion, razor, feminine pads, deodorant, toothbrush, toothpaste, toilet paper, liquid laundry soap, clothes pegs and clothesline (already mentioned under camping gear).

**Car Repair & Navigation:** Spare tire, jack and lug wrench, fix-a-flat, street and topographical maps, compass, extra motor oil, jumper cables, basic toolkit and battery-run air pump.

# List of Suggested Suppliers and Reading Material

**Note:** Although the author has studied, and in some cases ordered from the following suggested sites, it is always wise to do your own research for the best pricing and availability for your geographic location. At the time of the publication of *Survival: Prepare Before Disaster Strikes,* each site listed was operational.

### Suggested Courses

*YMCA*
http://www.ymca.net/find-your-y/

*Red Cross*
http://www.redcross.org/portal/site/en/menuitem.86f46a12f382290517a8f210b80f78a0/?vgnextoid=aea70c45f663b110VgnVCM10000089f0870aRCRD

### Emergency Kit Supplies

http://www.quakekare.com/emergency-survival-kits-c-1.html?gclid=CLTK4Pfv8aYCFQRubAodeUDuEw

http://www.survival-goods.com/

http://emergencykitsupplies.com/

http://www.emergencyanddisastersupplies.com/emergencykits

### First Aid Supplies

http://www.cprsavers.com/?source=GOOG&wcw=google&kw=first+aid+supply

http://www.first-aid-product.com/

## Emergency Plans and Utility Shut-Off

http://www.fema.gov/plan/prepare/plan.shtm

http://ready.adcouncil.org/beprepared/fep/index.jsp

http://www.doh.wa.gov/phepr/handbook/utility.htm

## Fire Extinguisher Basics

http://www.fireextinguisher.com/

## Chimney Fire Information

http://www.csia.org/HomeownerResources/ChimneySafetyInfo/Chimn
eyFireFacts/tabid/126/Default.aspx

## Wood Burning Devices & Hot Water Installation

http://woodheat.org/index.php?option=com_content&view=article&id
=32&Itemid=63

## Driving Safety and Emergency Preparedness

http://www.weather.com/ready/checklists/drivingChecklist.html

## EMP: Electromagnetic Pulse

http://afteremp.com/information/

## What to Do During Storms and Flooding

http://www.nws.noaa.gov/os/brochures.shtml

## Recommended Reference Books and Articles

*How to Stay Alive in the Woods* by Bradford Angier

*Nature's Garden: A Guide to Identifying, Harvesting, and Preparing Edible Wild Plants* by Samuel Thayer

*Edible Wild Plants: A North American Field Guide* by Thomas Elias and Peter Dykeman

*Ramifications of Cyber Attack on the U.S. Grid—Article*
http://www.shtfplan.com/headline-news/cyber-attack-on-us-grid-would-be-devastating-trojans-malware-trapdoors-already-exist_01162011

*Boy Scouts Handbook* Note: try to find an edition written before 1970 for best content.

*First Aid (American Red Cross Handbook) Responding to Emergencies*

*Hesparian Health Guides—some have free PDF downloads. Others may be available upon request*
http://hesperian.org/books-and-resources/

## Free Downloads

*Nuclear War Survival*
http://www.nukepills.com/docs/nuclear_war_survival_skills.pdf

## Blog and Websites for Survival/Preparedness Information

*Thousands of free articles related to preparedness and survival*
http://www.survivalblog.com/

*Get ready to learn and have some fun with survival*
http://www.preparednesspro.com/blog/

*Informative blog all about preparedness*
http://thesurvivalmom.com/

*Excellent info on survival related subjects*
http://suburbansurvivalist.wordpress.com/

*Offers great insight into gear and survival book reviews*
http://teotwawkiblog.blogspot.com/

*Offers a unique take on bugging out problems and solutions*
http://www.bugoutsurvival.com/

*Great how-to topics on subjects related to survival*
http://www.survivaltopics.com/

*Survival related downloads*
http://modernsurvivalonline.com/survival-database-downloads/

## Get Connected: Forums to Exchange Information and Ideas

*Find like-minded folks, post questions and share*
http://www.preppergroups.com/

## DIY Manual Washing Machine

http://www.off-grid.net/2010/04/22/diy-washing-machine-and-homemade-laundry-soap/

## DIY Outhouse

http://www.small-cabin.com/small-cabin-build-other-structures.html

## Potassium Iodide (KI) Suppliers & Potassium Iodate (K103)

http://www.cosmos.com.mx/pqs/4flf.htm

http://www.ki4u.com/products.htm#1

http://www.labdepotinc.com/c-164-laboratory-chemicals.php

http://www.baproducts.com/ki.htm

# Chapter 3

# Water Sources, Purification and Storage

*"We never know the worth of water till the well is dry."*
Thomas Fuller

The average person can survive without water for 2 days in temperatures of 120 degrees and 10 days in temperatures of 50 degrees. When you are active and exposed to hot weather, the body requires close to one gallon of water a day. Cold weather can be nearly as challenging because cold air dehydrates the body as you breathe. Cold also robs your body of moisture through exposed skin.

The bare minimum for water requirements in an emergency situation is 28 gallons a month per person. This is inclusive of two quarts of drinking water and two quarts of bathing and clean-up water. Considering the average person uses between 1,500 and 2,400 gallons of water each month during normal times, the estimate of 28 gallons is an admittedly frugal recommendation and is purely for bare necessity purposes due to storage issues. If you have your heart set on filling a bathtub now and then, you should store more. Much more!

At the very least, one month's worth of water should be stored for each member of your family or group, but that's with the proviso there is a nearby water source and you have a quality water purifier available to process water for drinking, cooking, and clean-up.

**Warning:** Even the best of water purifiers will **not** filter fallout material in contaminated water. Refer to *Fallout Filtering Methods* later in this chapter.

## Water Storage

It is important to store water safely, otherwise you could put aside enough water to fill an Olympic-sized swimming pool and still be outside the safe zone. The following are methods to safely store water for drinking:

### Chlorine Bleach

Bleach that contains a 5.25% solution of sodium hypochlorite and does not contain soap additives or phosphates can be added to water for long-term storage. Use a ratio of 1/8 teaspoon of chlorine bleach for each gallon of water.

### 2% Tincture of Iodine

Stored water requires 12 drops of iodine for each gallon of water. **Warning:** Pregnant women and those suffering with thyroid disease or other health risks should not drink water treated with iodine without first consulting a physician. If you are unsure whether or not you are allergic to iodine, do not use this method.

### Ion

Ion is another method to preserve water. It is made of stabilized oxygen. Use 20 drops of ion per gallon of water.

Water storage should be changed approximately every 6 months, but in an emergency, treated water that has been left in containers longer is still safe to drink. When stored water tastes flat, pour it from one container to another a few times. This will re-oxygenate the water and make it more palatable.

## Water Storage Methods

Water storage containers come in 5, 7, 15, and 55-gallon sizes and everything in between. If your budget has little wriggle room, you can store water in two-liter pop bottles. Do not store water in old milk cartons. They are biodegradable and will begin to break down within 6 months. Any leakage can destroy food storage items it comes in contact with.

No matter if your backyard butts up to one of the Great Lakes, or you are fortunate enough to have a well, it is advisable to keep 2 weeks worth of stored water in your home both for convenience sake and for the ability to remain in your home when conditions are unsafe. A few good examples would be a nuclear event or looting in your vicinity has reached dangerous levels.

## Alternate Water Sources

Be prepared for water supply lines to be disrupted during an emergency. It is important that you research your immediate vicinity for an alternate water source like a lake, river, creek, or even a stagnant pond, for stagnant pond water *can* be ran through a quality water filter for safe drinking water (Refer to the next section: Water Purifiers). With luck, you will find a water source close by because a 7-gallon container of water weighs 56 lbs. If you live a good distance away from a water source, shop around for a pull cart, or consider a less expensive child's wagon, as this will make hauling water much easier. Determine the easiest way to access the water source, so when the time comes, you will be prepared to get in and out with less effort.

If you live in a small space where storing water would be challenging or impossible, then it's time to get creative. A king-sized waterbed holds 180 gallons of water, a queen-size waterbed holds 158 gallons, and a twin size holds 90 gallons. As long as you have a water siphon, collapsible water containers, and bleach, iodine of tincture, or ion for purification, you have solved the problem of providing for the single most important item in your preparedness arsenal: water. At least for the short-term...

In an extreme emergency, you can consume the water stored in a hot water heater. Make sure the power is off before you begin, as hot water heaters are wired to 220. Next, turn off the water intake valve at the bottom of the heater. You may have to turn on a hot water faucet from somewhere else in the house to get the water to flow. Sediment may be found in the water, but in an emergency, letting it settle to the bottom of a container and purifying it will make it drinkable.

You can also access water from the water pipes in your house. To do this, turn on the faucet located at the highest level of your home. This will allow air to enter the plumbing and you can collect it from a faucet on the lowest level of your home.

In a real pinch, you can use the water stored in the reservoir of your toilet tank—not the bowl—which brings to mind the very best water purifier.

## Water Purifiers

Water purifier capabilities vary greatly. Be certain you purchase a water purifier capable of filtering out the following: pathogenic bacteria, parasites, herbicides, pesticides, organic solvents, VOCs, and heavy metals such as cadmium, chromium, copper, lead, mercury, aluminum as well as nitrates. They should also be capable of clearing out cloudiness, silt, sediment, foul tastes and odors.

The best water purifiers will do all this without removing the beneficial minerals your body needs. Clearly, this is a tall order and why this is an instance where you cannot afford to scrimp, as survival without a reliable source of water is an impossibility. I personally recommend either the Berkey or Katadyn. The manufacturer will tell you how many gallons can be processed though the water purifier before the filter(s) must be changed. You can calculate what your water purifier filter needs will be by adding the number of people in your family or group into monthly gallon requirements, then multiply that by the number of months you are planning for preparedness. Next, pencil in Murphy's Law, and throw in a few more filter replacements!

If you are a consummate procrastinator, and are caught in an emergency without a water purifier, or in the event of nuclear fallout where water purifiers are not sufficient, refer *Three Ways to Purify Water without a Water Purifier* and *Fallout Water Purification* found below.

## Three Ways to Purify Water without a Water Purifier

The following instructions are for purifying water from alternate sources once your water storage has been exhausted

In addition to having a bad odor and taste, contaminated water can contain microorganisms that cause diseases such as dysentery, cholera, typhoid and hepatitis. Because of this, you should purify all water of uncertain purity before using it for drinking, food preparation, or hygiene use.

There are several ways to purify water. Before purifying, let any suspended particles settle to the bottom, or strain the water through layers of paper towel or a clean, absorbent cloth.

Three easy purification methods are outlined below. These measures will kill microbes but will **not** remove other contaminants such as heavy metals, salts, most other chemicals, nor will it rid water of radioactive fallout.

## Purifying Water without a Commercial Water Filter

**Boiling** is the safest method for purifying water. Bring water to a rolling boil for at least one minute and let it cool. Boiled water will taste better if you put oxygen back into it by pouring it back and forth between two containers.

**Chlorine Bleach** can be used to kill microorganisms. Add 1/8 teaspoon of bleach to each gallon of water, stir and let stand for at least 30 minutes.

**Purification Tablets** release chlorine or iodine. They are inexpensive and available at most sporting goods stores and some drugstores. Follow the package directions. Usually one tablet is enough to purify 1 liter of water. Double the recommended dose for cloudy water.

## Water Distillation for Microbes, Heavy Metals, Salt and Chemicals

While the three methods described above will remove only microbes from water, the following purification method will remove microbes, heavy metals, salts and most chemicals.

Distillation involves boiling water and then collecting the vapor that condenses. The condensed vapor will not include salt and other impurities. To distill, fill a pot halfway with water. Tie a cup to the handle on the pot's lid, turning the lid upside down, so that the cup will hang right-side-up when the lid is upside-down. Put the lid on the pot (make sure the cup is not dangling into the water), and boil the water for 20 minutes. The water that drips from the lid into the cup is distilled.

## Fallout Water Purification

Water itself cannot become radioactive, but it can be contaminated by radioactive fallout material. For safe drinking water that may have been contaminated with fallout, follow the directions below:

Making a fallout water filter starts with two 5-gallon food storage buckets. You will need to punch holes in the bottom of one bucket to allow water to flow through into the next to capture the filtered water. Next, you will need to fill the bucket with 2 inches of soil (the more clay in the soil, the better). It's important to dig down past soil that could have come in contact with fallout, so dig down at least 4 inches, and preferably 6 inches, beneath the soil surface. Place a layer of clean towel with good absorbency properties that has been cut a little larger than the circumference of the bucket and place it on top of the soil. You can now use your handmade fallout water purifier by allowing water to flow through the purifier to the other bucket.

It is important to keep track of the amount of water that runs through a homemade fallout water filter because the soil and towel must be changed out after 50 quarts of water has been processed through it.

## Water Containment Systems

Large quantities of water can be stored through the use of a water containment system that captures rainwater from the roof. One inch of rainwater on a 20 foot by 20 foot roof can generate 1,200 gallons of water. The water is collected through gutters and downspouts that are routed into containment barrels.

It is possible to make your own inexpensively (instructions below), but you must be certain the barrels used are food grade quality and when purchasing used barrels, you need to verify they did not contain chemicals or other hazardous materials.

## DIY Water Containment System

Install a faucet near the base of a 55-gallon food grade plastic barrel, leaving enough room to draw water into a container. Once you've determined the placement where you will be installing the faucet, drill a one-inch hole. Now spread silicone around the threads of the faucet. Insert the faucet into the hole and secure it with a ¾ inch female adapter made of PVC.

At the top (not the lid) of the barrel, there needs to be an overflow hole. This is made by cutting a 2-inch hole with a hole saw. Now, cover it with window screen that's been cut a bit larger than the 2-inch hole size and secure it by using silicone sealant. The screen is meant to keep insects from entering your water barrel and contaminating the water.

Using a jigsaw cut a larger, 6-inch hole on the top of the barrel and cover it with window screen to keep debris and insects out. This hole is where the water that has been routed from the roof will enter the containment barrel.

Place the barrel directly under the downspout to collect rainwater. The water can then be diverted to a garden area, or saved for drinking and bathing. The downside of a water containment system is the size of the barrels, making them easy to spot for the casual observer, tipping your hand to your preparedness should you live in a populated area. Their upside is they will extend your drinking water without having to haul it from an open water source. Check your area's annual rainfall to make sure the expenditure of a water containment system is worthwhile before purchasing.

**Warning:** Water containment barrels cannot be used in below-freezing conditions, as the barrels will expand upon freezing and split. At the time of this writing Washington, Utah, and Colorado state officials have decided that rainwater collection is illegal. Apparently these States have gone on record by claiming the rain "belongs to someone else." Who that someone was is anyone's guess! Expect to see playhouses and sheds go up whose roofs connect to downspouts.

## Water Wells

If you are fortunate enough to have a well, you should plan for a manual hand pump. That way, in a grid-down situation when your electric pump is rendered useless, you won't be looking longingly at your well house, water just beneath your feet, with no earthly way to retrieve it. In northern climates, look for a frost-free model. They are available online and at hardware and home improvement stores. Quality manual pumps don't come cheap, however. After researching which style worked best for my area in North Idaho, where winters often bring sub-zero temperatures, it lead me to a frost-free model that cost $1,500.

Just after emptying my bank account for that frost-free manual hand pump, I stumbled upon a water containment cylinder online at Lehman's for a mere $49. It holds just under two gallons of water and has to be lowered into the well with a rope, but hey! At least a person can collect water without having to break the piggybank.

## Do-It-Yourself Water Well

If you're interested in digging your own well, go to Fred Dungan's site "An Inexpensive, Do-It-Yourself Water Well" that gives very thorough step-by-step instructions on a DIY well for under $500: http://www.fdungan.com/well.htm

# List of Suggested Suppliers and Reading Material

**Note:** Although the author has studied, and in some cases ordered from the following suggested sites, it is always wise to do your own research for the best pricing and availability for your geographic location. At the time of the publication of *Survival: Prepare Before Disaster Strikes,* each site listed was operational.

## An Inexpensive, Do-It-Yourself Water Well & Hand Pump

http://www.fdungan.com/well.htm

## Berkey Water Purifiers

http://www.morethanalive.com/Berkey_Water_Filters?gclid=CI_okt6t 86YCFRxqgwod5BsdGg

## Katadyn Water Purifiers

http://www.katadyn.com/usen/

## Roof Rainwater Containment Systems

http://www.gardeners.com/Rain-Barrel-How-To/5497,default,pg.html

## Water Bladder Containment System

http://store.interstateproducts.com/water_bladders.htm

## Water Barrels & Storage Tanks

http://www.plastic-mart.com/?gclid=CNyize6w86YCFQUSbAod N3wNBg

http://www.bayteccontainers.com/waterbarrels.html

http://www.plastic-mart.com/?gclid=CNyize6w86YCFQUSbAod
N3wNBg

## Manual Water Pumps

http://www.solar4power.com/solar-power-water-pump.html

http://www.do-it-yourself-pumps.com/handpumps.htm

http://www.survivalunlimited.com/deepwellpump.htm

http://www.oasispumps.com/pumps.html

## Lehman's Galvanized Well Bucket ITEM# 550202

http://www.lehmans.com/?partner_id=bcbgoog&gclid=CO6Cnom386
YCFQN7gwodp1utIA

## Ion (Stabilized Oxygen) Suppliers

http://www.yourfoodstorage.com/product/12770666

http://www.survivalunlimited.com/waterstorage.htm

## Water Purification Tablets

http://www.globalhydration.com/aquatabs-water-purification-
tablets.htm

## Important Information on Water Purification and Diseases

http://zenbackpacking.net/WaterFilterPurifierTreatment.htm

## 2% Tincture of Iodine

http://reviews.walgreens.com/2001/prod1544039/apothecary-iodine-
tincture-2-usp-reviews/reviews.htm

# Chapter 4

# First Be S.A.F.E.

*"It is not the strongest of the species that survive,*
*nor the most intelligent that survives.*
*It is the one that is the most adaptable to change."*
Charles Darwin

In a crisis, expect grocery store shelves to be laid bare within twelve hours. Even during a mildly disruptive event like an advancing winter storm, staples fly off the shelves at warp speed and within three days, grocery store shelves are picked clean. We have all seen the reports on the evening news: people scrambling to grab staples and bottled water ahead of the snowfall. Then the storm passes, the roads are cleared, truckers are able to make deliveries and the residents' concerns over empty pantries dissolve to a distant memory.

Good luck with that when a crisis strikes! Truckers will be stuck in gridlock as people flee to safety, roads will be closed or impassable in places, and services will most definitely be disrupted.

Gas stations, grocery stores, electricity, phone lines, heat and water, are all part of everyday life we take for granted. But with regards to survival, it is safest to assume we will be without these basic services for at least a short duration, and possibly the long-term.

At the very crux of preparedness is the determination to survive. This is much more likely with a mindset of independence, a can-do attitude and a realistic plan to provide the basics: food, water, and shelter. At its essence, preparedness is a preemptive strike against helplessness. We plan for weddings and other important events, don't we? Then why not plan for food, water, and shelter? The wonderful thing about preparedness is the peace of mind it brings. And the results are tangible—inflation-proof food storage at a time when food prices continue to skyrocket.

## The S.A.F.E. Principle

Preparedness is much like a puzzle, with each puzzle piece fitting cohesively against the next. Omit a piece, and the end result will be about as effective as putting lipstick on a pit bull. It won't work!

At the beginning stages of preparedness, think in terms of manual appliances for basic survival. Later, when basic preparedness goods have been put aside, you can get as shopaholic as you'd like, maybe buy a gas-run generator or a chainsaw. Now that's fun for the whole family...until your stash of gasoline runs dry.

Nearly 81% of the population lives in urban locations for good reason: it's where the jobs are. If you are among this 81%, your challenges will be greater during a crisis than for those living in rural locations. You will not have a well, and may not have a yard for gardening. The most concerning aspect of urban living is dense population, for with crowded conditions comes the inevitability of crime—most notably looting. The S.A.F.E. Principle takes this in to consideration.

Even those living in a rural location will want to review the S.A.F.E. Principle, for we have all grown used to cushy lives. Your success of surviving a crisis does not rest solely on having a garden and a well, although you will be thankful you have them. Review this section to be sure all the pieces fit together for a preparedness plan that will succeed.

**S** – Space

**A** – Ability

**F** – Finances

**E** – Environment

To have one element of the S.A.F.E. Principle, for instance the Finances to buy 25 lb bags of dry beans, without the other— the Ability to cook them—equates to failure. Be brutally honest with yourself. If you must, step outside yourself and view your storage space, abilities, finances, and environment in the third person. If you feel yourself rationalizing away the negatives, push the inclination aside and get back to the business of evaluating your circumstances with brutal honesty. By reviewing the S.A.F.E. Principle, and by utilizing the process of elimination, you will be able to determine the best choices to bring you to self-sufficiency in no time, whether your assessment leads you to MRE's (meals ready to eat), bulk food storage, canned goods, or a mixture of all three.

When preparing for a crisis, do not depend on utilities! Okay, now I'm harping...but let's face it, we are spoiled, and used to our creature comforts. Toss comfort out of your head, so your preparedness plan doesn't have so many holes it could be used in place of a colander. The same goes for dependency on natural gas and propane. In other words, do not expect to be able to cook on your electric or gas stove. And forget about running water. If the electrical grid crashes, so might your local water district's ability to deliver water to your home. In a flood or earthquake, the water supply may not be safe to drink without purification, even when you can draw it from your faucet.

Keeping all the above in mind, have a look at the S.A.F.E. Principle to determine your best approach to preparedness.

## Space

I've yet to meet the person who feels they have enough storage space. With regards to food and water storage, space is important. So is ingenuity. Although basements and root cellars are ideal for bulk food storage, if you have neither, then space can be found under beds, in closets, in and above kitchen cupboards, coat closets, and guest-rooms. However, if your available space is the size of a postage stamp, MRE's or canned goods might be the best food storage choice. Of course, you could always copy a friend of mine who took two plain 55-gallon trash barrels, filled one with rice and other with beans, and hid them with designer fabric that looked suspiciously like slub silk—I was afraid to ask.

Bulk foods take quite a bit of storage space, and to get optimal shelf life from bulk foods, they should be stored in a dark, cool, and moisture free location.

If your home has a basement, or a free room that meets the criteria for bulk foods, then your choice may be centered more on personal preference.

## Ability

Does your idea of cooking require reservations? If so, head straight for MRE's, canned goods, or a combination of both. At the onset, MRE's may appear expensive, and they do cost more, but maybe not as much as you might think. When you pencil in the cost of cooking fuel, spices and condiments typically used with cooking bulk food, and figure in the price of storage containers, the difference is not as great as it might appear at first glance.

## Finances

Lately, many of us have found ourselves shouting: "Where's the money?" when we dare check our bank balance. If this is you, don't panic. There are ways to save 50%-90% when you shop smart. It's not unlike a 75% off sale at Cabella's; only in this case, you are shopping for canned goods and bulk foods. Trust me, you'll never see anyone get wrestled to the floor over a can of creamed spinach like you would over the bling of a camp stove. There simply isn't all that much competition for canned goods and bags of rice and beans, and soon, you'll be the proud owner of a basement full of food storage.

For most of us with less than desirable pocketbooks, self-sufficiency starts one trip to the store at a time. But if your foreseeable future does not allow for extra food storage, there are workarounds.

If you have determined your best approach are MRE's or canned meals for their convenience, but your pocketbook disagrees, think outside the box and visit a local Dollar Store for ready-to-eat canned goods. Recently, Dollar Stores have recognized the need for affordable food and have begun to add to their canned goods shelves. Start there.

If all else fails, get together with loved ones and make a plan. My personal experience might serve as an example. In exchange for my purchasing preparedness goods and supplies, several members of my extended family helped to install a wood-burning cook stove in my cabin, and they built a chicken coop, and for good measure, built a goat enclosure. Next, land was cleared for a garden. The labor costs that were saved went straight back into the food storage and preparedness goods. Now when crisis strikes, we will survive on this small homestead with a well, a wood-burning cook stove, goats, chickens, a garden, and food storage enough for 22 people.

My point is it isn't always about cash. If you find yourself in a similar situation, set a plan in motion with loved ones that distributes the workload vs. cash outlay. This will allow you to contribute towards preparedness to everyone's benefit.

You might also try lowering your monthly grocery bill for less expensive items and put the savings towards food storage. I know food prices have soared lately, but shaving off a little here and there adds up. You might also look around and see if you have something of value you could do without, sell it, and use that money for food supplies. A high-ticket item like a jet ski that may find its way into the water a few times in summer is a likely candidate. When selling a possession equates to enough food storage for survival, it's worth consideration. After all, even with a generous sprinkling of salt and pepper and a dash of A-1 sauce, you can't eat a jet ski! It all comes down to how committed you are to preparing. Think about it. What can you give up in order to prepare?

# Environment

The human race is adaptable, and many times, we grow complacent with our surroundings. Given enough time, we will likely get used to crowded conditions and the hustle and bustle of living in a dense population. But for the purposes of preparedness, crowded conditions are an important aspect to take into consideration when planning for survival.

Environment dictates decisions with regards to cooking methods. That, in turn, leads to what type of food storage will best fit your needs. To reach a decision takes a multifaceted assessment of location, safety, and population. Ask yourself if your location is likely to be safe in a disaster. If you live in a city or a suburb with a dense population, the answer is most likely no. During a time of upheaval, people will take to the streets for survival, and rest assured, there will be looters among them. If your plan involves cooking outdoors over an open fire pit or using an outdoor BBQ in a populated area, go directly to a plan B. Cooking smells and smoke generated from cooking will act as a beacon of opportunity for anyone with a growling stomach.

Under these conditions, it is safest to confine cooking to indoor spaces. BBQ's produce high levels of carbon monoxide and are not designed for indoor use. An alternative is a camp stove, as long as you have windows that can be opened, for they also produce unhealthy levels of carbon monoxide without proper ventilation. Because of this, you must ask yourself if it's worth the risk to advertise to neighbors and passersby that you have provisions. Hunger is a strong foe. Keep that in mind when planning for alternate cooking.

You might want to investigate solar cookers if your climate zone has the necessary sunlight. Their benefits are low cooking odors and they are not dependent upon the electrical grid.

It is likely that for those living in populated urban areas, MRE's, prepared canned meals, and canned fruits and vegetables are the safest choice. Most MRE's are made to cook in their own jackets and will not produce cooking odors. Just as important, MRE's are portable, and should your location become unsafe, and you are forced to relocate, they are much easier to move than 40 lb buckets of beans and rice from one location to another.

Lest I sound as if I am a majority shareholder in an MRE supplier, my personal choice was a mixture of bulk, dehydrated, and canned goods. The decision was made easier when I determined, early on, to move to a rural setting. If I hadn't reached a point in life where I was confident in making a living from writing that could be done from the edge of the wilderness, I'd still be living in the city and my choice for food storage would have been MRE's.

For those living in rural areas, cooking over an open fire pit or with wood-burning fireplaces, fireplace inserts, Sheppard's stoves, or wood burning cook stoves (more on these in Chapter 4) offer excellent alternative cooking methods and will allow you to cook whatever food storage you like. Cast iron Dutch ovens and pans are great for cooking bulk foods, including baked goods and breads.

The downside to these alternative cooking methods is they require a boatload of storage space for seasoned firewood that must be stored out of sight to avoid looting. This necessity, along with outside venting requirements and cooking odors limits the possibilities for those who live in urban environments.

Even though rural settings offer a wide range of choices for cooking and food storage, keep in mind if you have neighbors living nearby who are not prepared, you can expect a knock on your door. This is especially true when cooking outdoors. The enticing aroma of beans simmering over an open fire will find its way around the neighborhood.

## Even Preparedness Has a "Gray" Area

As you began to plan your strategy for food storage, you'll need to decide whether or not you'll be including extended family members, friends, neighbors or strangers in need. Helping others is a righteous thing, but it will put a drain on your food storage. Plan ahead!

If you can afford to help others, take into consideration cooking needs. Handing someone dry beans and rice when they have no means to cook them will lead to another decision: to invite them to stay, or send them off to an uncertain future. If possible, put aside extra canned goods or MRE's that do not have to be cooked for such emergencies.

# Chapter 5

# Which Cooking Method is Best for You?

*"Life is an error-making and an error-correcting process,
and nature in making man's papers will grade him for wisdom as
measured by survival and by the quality of life of those who survive."*
Jonas Sulk

Because of the importance of selecting the right alternate cooking method for your circumstances, this chapter is devoted to a detailed breakdown of various cooking methods; the pros and the cons.

**Note**: If you determine that a wood burning cooking alternative best suits your needs, plan for a reliable tree-felling axe that will allow you to stay on top of your firewood needs. Always have fireplace flues checked for built-up creosote to avoid chimney fires.

All wood burning devices will need a large amount of seasoned wood that should be stored safely out of sight to avoid looting.

For those who live in regions with plenty of trees, a wood-burning cooking alternative is likely to be your best choice for convenience and sustainability. Just make sure to have a backup plan for those hot summer days when cooking inside would heat up living spaces to unbearable levels.

If your preparedness plan includes home canning, where temperatures must be controlled, a wood-burning or propane-run stove will be the best choice.

**Warning:** Propane and most camp stove fuels must be stored outdoors in structures such as a shed or garage, away from the home and heaters or furnaces and other devices with an open flame.

# Outdoor Barbeques

Most of us have barbeques that can provide a short-term solution for cooking during an emergency. Problem is, they won't work for the long-term.

**Limitations:** Whether a barbeque uses briquettes or propane, they must never be used indoors, as they produce unhealthy levels of carbon monoxide and are not safe for indoor use, even with ventilation. During a protracted emergency, when services may be down indefinitely, your ability to cook will be a race against the clock; one that winds down the moment your fuel source is exhausted.

A barbeque is not the best choice for those living in an urban setting because of the cooking odors they generate. They also require a large storage space for briquettes or propane.

# Camp Stoves

Camp stoves have many advantages, starting with price and the adaptability for indoor cooking. They come in all sizes: single, double, and triple burner models; some even come with ovens. They use a variety of fuel sources: propane, butane, kerosene, denatured alcohol, unleaded gasoline, leaded gas, and white gas. Some camp stoves have been designed to operate using more than one fuel source. Smaller models use sterno, hexamine tabs, or trioxane bars.

**Limitations:** You must have adequate ventilation to use a camp stove indoors. Without ventilation, they must be used outdoors to avoid carbon monoxide poisoning. Camp stoves require propane or other fuels which may not be renewable.

# Fireplaces

You may already have a fireplace that can be utilized for cooking, much like you would prepare food over a campfire. You will need a grate, cast iron cookware, and a secure supply of firewood. Although a fireplace is not the most efficient way to heat a home, during an emergency, they will heat a portion of your living space by cording the area off with heavy blankets hung from floor to ceiling.

If you have never used a reflector oven, it's time to go online in search of one. Made of metal, these simple, open-concept ovens are wonderful to cook baked goods with by placing them in front of a fireplace, fireplace insert, or an open fire pit.

## Wood-Burning Fireplace Inserts

Fireplace inserts offer maximized efficiency for heating the home and serve a dual purpose, a way to cook your food storage. Cooking with a wood-burning insert is best done with cast iron Dutch ovens, and cast iron pans. Cooking entails placing your cookware directly on or over hot embers, just as you would with an open fire pit. Baking can be done in a Dutch oven or with a reflector oven. When using a reflector oven, you will need to keep the door of your fireplace insert ajar, at least partially, so your baked goods will receive enough heat.

## Open Fire Pits

Cast iron Dutch ovens and pots and pans are the perfect solution for cooking over an open fire pit. With practice, Dutch ovens will cook most of the foods you're used to cooking on your kitchen stove, including baked goods such as bread, biscuits, and cakes. There are numerous cookbooks (categorized as camping, or "roughing it" cookbooks) that have excellent recipes for fire pit cooking, some of which are supplied at the end of this chapter.

Just as with fireplace cooking, using a reflector oven when cooking over an open fire pit will provide bake goods. Cooking tripods can be purchased for use with fire pit cooking that are capable of holding cookware over an open flame by a chain that can be adjusted up and down for more controlled cooking.

## Wood Heat Stoves

Wood burning stoves can be used for cooking, either on top or in the firebox over hot coals. Many who live in rural areas already have a wood burning heat stove. It is advisable to have the chimney checked for creosote buildup if this hasn't already been done. Some models of wood burning stoves come with water reservoirs, which comes in handy when you want hot water for cleanup and bathing.

## Propane Cook Stoves

Propane cook stoves are already popular with many people who live in rural settings. When considering a propane cook stove for survival purposes, look into having one of the larger propane tanks delivered to your location if you haven't already done so. Normally, propane companies will provide the tank with a small deposit and will fill them on their routine runs. Propane has the advantage of providing both heating and cooking. A real plus is propane stoves do not generate excessive heat in summertime. Refrigeration is also possible with propane.

Used propane stoves, heaters, and refrigerators can be found in the classifieds, craigslist and secondhand stores. You can also check with motor home and camper dealerships for smaller used appliances.

**Limitations:** Propane is expensive and the price just keeps going up. The biggest concern with propane is similar to camp stoves: they can be relied on only as long as the fuel (in this case propane) holds out. For this reason, they are not as sustainable as a wood burning device for those who live in areas where wood is plentiful. There may be restrictions with regards to storing large tanks of propane in your area. In a worst case scenario, above ground propane tanks are not impervious to bullets and can be a liability. If possible, consider buying a large tank and burying it for safety.

# Solar Cookers

For those living in sunny climates, solar cookers can't be beat. In an urban setting, their benefits are fewer cooking odors, and they can be placed on decks and patios that receive full sunlight.

Some solar cookers can reach incredible temperatures—up to 400 degrees. They must be moved with the movement of the sun to generate the most heat possible. Both urban dwellers and those living in the country can benefit from solar cookers, as they do not require a fuel source.

There are many cookbooks available on cooking with solar. A list has been provided at the end of this chapter.

**Limitations:** Solar cookers won't work for home canning. A solar cooker is completely dependent on sunlight. For those living in a northern climate, their use is limited.

# Wood Burning Cook Stoves and Sheppard's Stoves

Wood burning cook stoves typically come with a higher price tag, but these workhorses are the choice of many who are interested in long-term, sustainable cooking. They can also heat a small house. Purchased new or used, some models come with water reservoirs for hot water for household cleanup and bathing. If your pocketbook shrivels at the thought of purchasing new, it is possible to retrofit a water reservoir for a used wood cook stove at the time of installation. However, check with an expert before purchase to verify a retrofit is possible.

If you plan to home can, a wood cook stove is capable of maintaining the heat needed to put up food safely. This will take practice—lots of practice—unless you've already cooked with one.

Wood burning cook stoves and Sheppard stoves (mentioned below) are available at retail locations and can be found online. For used stoves, try antique stores, craigslist, and your local classifieds. Be sure the stove is in working order before purchasing, as replacement parts can be difficult to find and repairs are usually expensive.

Sheppard stoves (also included with this group are outfitter's stoves, cylinder stoves, and wall tent stoves) rely on firewood or coal. They come with or without separate ovens that are mounted in the chimneystack and some models offer water reservoirs. Depending on the model and style, cooking is done either on the top of its flat surface, the firebox, or a separate oven. With the use of a cast iron Dutch oven or cast iron pans, they are a good choice for cooking food storage. For those who prefer to remain mobile, some Sheppard stoves are available in lighter-weight models that collapse for portability. Compared to wood burning cook stoves, Sheppard stoves are less expensive.

There are numerous cookbooks for cooking with wood burning cook stoves and Sheppard's stoves offering down-home recipes that are user-friendly for cooking with bulk food storage. If you already own either a wood burning cook stove or a Sheppard's stove, have the chimney checked for creosote deposits if you haven't already done so.

**Note**: When estimating the cost of wood burning cook stoves and Sheppard stoves, be sure to price out the cost of an up-to-code stovepipe. After purchasing a 30's era, no-frills wood burning cook stove for $250, I was disappointed to discover that an up-to-code stovepipe cost $400. Other cost considerations are cement board to protect the wall behind the stove and a hearth to protect the floor. Taking shortcuts is not advisable. Not only would your homeowners insurance deny any claim caused by unsafe installation, during a crisis local fire departments will already have their hands full and may not be able to respond to an emergency call.

## Pellet Stoves

Pellet stoves are not the best route to go for either heating or cooking. To find the space to put enough pellets aside for any length of time would be overwhelming, plus pellets aren't renewable. Another drawback is their dependency on electricity to keep the fan going and to dump the pellets.

## Natural Gas Stoves & Fireplaces

Sadly, neither natural gas stoves nor natural gas fireplaces have anything to do with survival. They are entirely dependent on a steady, reliable supply of natural gas—not a given during an emergency.

## Electric Stoves

I doubt you have to guess what I'm about to say about electric stoves. Without electricity, you won't be cooking a thing! I am certain most of us have experienced power outages and suffered the frustration of not being able to cook. Now multiply that frustration by weeks, or months, and you'll arrive at the reason why an electric stove is not the best option.

For those of you who plan to run your electric stove with a gas-run generator, please consider an alternate cooking source just in case your gasoline storage isn't enough to see you through an extended crisis.

## Lesson Learned

In the Introduction, I promised to share my mistakes so that you might avoid doing something similar. My biggest blunder happened many years ago. It was a shinny new camp stove that had all the bells and whistles, including a small oven.

It was while searching for an adapter that would handle a couple of 100 lb propane tanks (to add to the 80 small camp-size propane tanks I'd already purchased) when it hit me. Propane is not renewable. In that split second of lucidity, my $250 "solution" to cook for my family evaporated.

My plan did not take into account that gas stations might not be open for business to refill the propane tanks. The reason for my lapse in judgment was simple. I hadn't wrapped my mind around a time when life as I knew it might not exist.

The moral? When planning for something as important as survival, plan for the worst and hope for the best.

# List of Suggested Suppliers and Reading Material

**Note:** Although the author has studied, and in some cases ordered from the following suggested sites, it is always wise to do your own research for the best pricing and availability for your geographic location. At the time of the publication of *Survival: Prepare Before Disaster Strikes,* each site listed was operational.

## Camping Equipment

*Cabelas Camp Stoves, Cylinder & Sheepherder's Stoves, Fire-Pit Tripods & Cast Iron Cookware*
http://www.cabelas.com/ghome.jsp?rid=20&WT.srch=1&WT.tsrc=PP
C&WT.mc_id=58000000000776350&WT.z_mc_id1=70785693

*Alpine Camping Supply*
http://www.alpinecampingsupply.com/

## Cast Iron Cookware

*Lodge Cast Iron*
http://www.lodgemfg.com/

*Iron Pots Depot*
http://www.ironpotsdepot.com/?source=adwords&gclid=CNHE_bWB
9aYCFQkSbAodsTyDCA

*Agri Supply*
http://www.agrisupply.com/cast-iron-cookware/c/6000136/c2c/sc/

## Sheppard's Stoves & Wall Tent Stoves

*AAOOB Sheppard Stoves*
http://www.aaoobfoods.com/shepherdstoves.htm

*Wall Tent Shop*
http://www.walltentshop.com/CatStoves.html

## Wood-Burning Fireplace Inserts & Wood Heat Stoves

*Lowes*
http://www.lowes.com/SearchCatalogDisplay?Ntt=fire+place+insert&storeId=10151&N=0&langId=-1&catalogId=10051&rpp=24

*Home Depot*
http://www.homedepot.com/?cm_mmc=SEM|RPM|ST_Branded|GGL_2881&skwcid=TC|13614|home%20depot||S|e|6468551964

*Vermont Castings*
http://www.vermontcastings.com/

## Wood Cook Stoves

*Antique Stoves*
http://www.antiquestoves.com/general%20store/generalstore.index.htm

*Lehman's*
http://www.lehmans.com/store/Stoves___Cook_Stoves?Args=&partner_id=COUNTRYLIFE/

*Obadiah's Woodstoves*
http://www.woodstoves.net/cookstoves.htm

## Propane Refrigerators and Ranges

http://www.adventurerv.net/major-appliances-oven-amp-range-c-24_86.html

http://www.pplmotorhomes.com/parts/rv-stoves-ovens-microwaves-parts-1.htm?source=google&gclid=CIfW3fbc9KYCFRg8gwodlAmuHA

http://www.lpappliances.com/

http://propaneapp.server101.com/Propane_Range.htm

## Solar Cookers

http://shop.solardirect.com/index.php?cPath=24_81&gclid=CJubtt3h9
KYCFRRqgwodum2-HA

http://www.solarcooker-at-cantinawest.com/buy-a-solar-cooker.html

## Camp Ovens

http://www.wisementrading.com/outdoorcooking/outdoorbaking.htm

http://www.coleman.com/coleman/colemancom/detail.asp?product_id
=5010D700T&categoryid=27400

## Reflector Oven Suppliers

http://www.mainemade.com/members/profile.asp?ID=2541

http://www.poleandpaddle.com/reflectorovens.html

## Recommended Reading

*How Solar Cookers Work—Article*
http://solarcookers.org/basics/how.html

## Do-It-Yourself Resources

*DIY Build a Solar Cooker*
http://solarcooking.org/plans/

*DIY How to Build Your Own Solar Food Cookers and Food Dryer*
http://www.builditsolar.com/Projects/Cooking/cooking.htm

*Plans and Instructions to Build a Reflector Oven*
http://www.kayak2go.com/reflectoroven.PDF

## Dutch Ovens, Reflector Oven and Solar Cooker Recipes

*Great Reflector Oven Recipes: Boys Life, Outdoors*
http://boyslife.org/outdoors/outdoorarticles/12765/great-reflector-oven-recipes/

*What's Cooking America—Lots of Cast Iron Recopies; Meals, Baked Goods, Desserts*
http://whatscookingamerica.net/CastIronRecipes.htm

*Care and Cooking with Dutch Ovens and Many Recipes*
http://papadutch.home.comcast.net/~papadutch/

*Recipes From Scratch: 100's of Dutch Oven Recipes*
http://www.recipesfromscratch.com/dutch/index.htm

*The Net Woods Virtual Campsites: Outdoor and Dutch Oven Recipes*
http://www.netwoods.com/d-cooking.html

*Solar Cooker Supplier/Recipes*
http://www.cookwiththesun.com/recipes.htm

*Solar Oven Society Recipes*
http://www.solarovens.org/recipes/

# Chapter 6

# Calculating & Storing Preparedness Foods

*"Despair is most often the offspring of ill-preparedness."*
Don Williams

It's time to calculate your food storage and I hope you'll forgive me for starting off with a bit of nagging. Have you calculated how many people you'll be preparing for? Can't make up your mind if Aunt Martha deserves your help after what she said last Christmas? Sadly, most of us have an Aunt Martha, but you'll need to decide, because it's time to fill those storage shelves and you can't do that until you know how many you will be shopping for.

Most of us don't have the cash flow to purchase one year's worth of food storage all at once, but judging from the rising food prices, you will be further ahead by purchasing as much as you can and build from there. However, if your budget can only handle a few days or weeks of food storage, you are still way ahead of most of the populace. Don't beat yourself up over timelines, but do keep your eye on the target.

Deluxe or Basic?

There are varying beliefs with regards to how in-depth food storage should be. Some feel it's best to store a large variety of foods with plenty of varying textures and flavors as well as comfort foods. Others recommend the basics like beans and rice and canned or dehydrated fruits and vegetables.

This issue is a toughie, for there is no "right answer". Preparedness is not one size fits all. It must take into consideration a person's finances, as well as who is being provide for. Are there children involved, or is your group made up of adults? What about the physiological make-up of the group…are these folks perfectly happy with a bowl of oatmeal at breakfast time, or do they slather caviar on little wedges of toast for breakfast? The caviar group, by the way, need to pony up on the cost of storage food! On top of that, they are going to have to learn to lower their expectations a bit.

When children are involved, a well-rounded storage plan that has a variety of flavors and textures that includes comfort foods is the safest approach to help boost a child's appetite. Otherwise Appetite Fatigue might be the result and they may choose hunger over another bowl of beans and rice. This will be discussed at more length in Chapter 7, *Avoiding Common Pitfalls*.

If, however, your family or group members are made up of adults, eating basics will suffice; at least at first. Later, once the basics have been purchased, variety and texture can be layered into your food storage plan.

For tight budgets, having "survival" foods means just what it says, survival! We can survive on beans and rice, and canned vegetables and fruits. There are other inexpensive foods that can be added to basic food storage like peanut butter and jam and tuna fish that are tasty and also provide necessary protein.

Free food storage calculators can be found online. Several sites have been listed at the end of this chapter. By entering the number of people you are providing for along with the number of months you plan to prepare for, you will be supplied with recommended basic food storage items and their amounts. But before your curiosity gets the best of you and you go in search of a food calculator, allow me to offer a warning: Do not let yourself go into meltdown when you get your answer! Remember, this is under optimal conditions. The first time I calculated my family's food storage needs, I slammed down the lid of my laptop at the injustice of it all.

Here's an example: As I was purchasing food storage for twenty-two people (I have a large extended family living close by), 800 pounds of powdered milk was recommended for one year's food storage. At the time powdered milk where I routinely buy dehydrated and freeze-dried food sold for $60 per case (6 # 10 cans). The total weight per case was 24 pounds. With these calculations, 800 pounds of milk substitute would have cost $990.

*No way* could I afford to pay nearly $1,000 for one item on a long, long list. It occurred to me, as it will you, these calculations are for survival in a perfect world, and we are not talking about a perfect world when disaster strikes. My decision? I bought several cases of powdered milk for the children in the family. The rest of us will be drinking water or powdered fruit drinks with the occasional glass of powdered milk. The moral here is do not let your journey overwhelm you. Food storage is not an exact science and you may decide to exclude more expensive items and replace them with vitamin and mineral supplements.

## Storing Food

How you store your food is yet another piece of the puzzle. When putting provisions aside, it is extremely important to protect bulk items such as beans, rice, flour, cornmeal, rolled oats, and wheat in containers with impenetrable lids.

Opaque buckets work well for this, as light is storage food's enemy and it will shorten the lifespan of your bulk storage food. You can purchase food-quality buckets for $7.00 to $10.00 each, but if you are on a budget, 5 gallon paint buckets with tight-fitting lids will suffice and are available at the big box hardware stores. I purchase mine at Home Depot. At the time of this writing, they cost $3 each; much cheaper than specialized buckets sold by food suppliers. To make sure a bucket is safe for food storage, turn it upside down and look for the triangle. Inside that triangle should have #2 and either HDPE or Poly Ethylene stamped within it. When in doubt, contact the manufacturer, or research it online. Whatever you do, do not store food in buckets that once contained unsafe chemicals or other hazardous materials. Make sure to purchase a lid opener, so you won't find yourself in a WWF wrestling match every time you need a little flour or sugar.

A real budget saver is contacting restaurants, ice cream shops, delis, and bakeries. They go through a tremendous amount of buckets and many times they give buckets away for free. Always double-check they held only food, and wash them thoroughly with soap and hot water before storing food in them.

It is important to line your buckets with food-grade Mylar bags before filling them. This will add a protective layer to keep moisture out—one of the worst offenders of the shelf life for any food. For the budget-conscience, Glad trash bags can be used. Up to this writing, they are not treated with pesticides.

Large outdoor trash containers work well for storing larger quantities of bulk items such as wheat, beans and rice. Be certain to purchase food-grade bags large enough to accommodate a trash container's larger size. The lids should be sealed with duct tape in order to keep pests and insects out.

Stackable tubs work well for storing items such as boxed goods and spices packaged in cardboard or otherwise flimsy containers that tend to attract rodents and insects. All tubs are not created equally. If you find the lids do not fit tightly enough, duct tape will solve the issue.

It is possible to extend the shelf life of your bulk storage by placing several oxygen absorbers in with storage food. Place an oxygen absorber once the container is 1/3 full, another when it is 2/3 full, and another at the top of the filled container. This will help control moisture. Oxygen absorbers are available online, or you can check with local health food stores. Once opened, they must be used immediately.

Bay leaves will stop insects from invading bulk storage such as beans, rice, and flour. Line the bucket with a food-quality bag and fill the bucket 1/3 full and add 3 to 4 dry bay leaves. Add another 1/3 of the bulk food into the bucket along with 3 to 4 bay leaves. When you've added the remaining 1/3 of the bulk food, include the last 3 to 4 bay leaves on top and close the bucket with a tight-fitting lid. It should be noted that some people have reported that although their food storage remained bug free, after a period of time, they could taste traces of bay leaf when cooking with their bulk foods.

Another solution for insect control is to place a 1/4 lb chunk of dry ice in the bottom of the storage bucket, then fill with bulk food such as beans, rice, corn or wheat, and place the lid on firmly, but don't permanently seal, as gasses need room to expand. After two hours, the lid can then be sealed permanently. This method fills air pockets with $CO_2$ gas and will typically will kill insects and discourage egg laying.

Make sure to mark your storage containers with the purchase date and the contents with indelible marker pen, facing out, where you can clearly read it. Times of crisis come with enough stress. To have to open container after container in search of a particular staple would make even the sanest of us go postal!

The date is especially important with regards to shelf life. Always consume your food storage before its shelf life has expired, and replace it as soon as possible—otherwise known as rotation. Detailed shelf life charts can be found online and are supplied at the end of this chapter.

Light, moisture, and temperature (including temperature fluctuations) are the enemy of stored food. If possible, store your provisions in a dark, cool, moisture-free location where the temperature stays at 70 degrees or below—the cooler, the better—but never below freezing. Obvious choices for storage are basements and root cellars. If you will be storing bulk items on an earth floor or on cement, lay pallets on the floor first so your bulk containers will not sweat, causing moisture to build up. Wooden pallets are sometimes available for free at building sites and hardware stores. Craigslist is another place to locate free pallets. If your food storage is in a space that might be penetrable by rodents, it is advisable to sprinkle rock sulfur in any cracks or openings where they might get in.

## Extending the Shelf Life of Storage Foods

Determining the shelf life of foods can be admittedly frustrating.

It's likely that for as many sites you go to for advice on the shelf life of a particular food, you will get that number of conflicting answers. This issue is discussed at greater length in Chapter 8, *Repeat After Me: I Will Spend No More Than Necessary!* But no matter which authority you put your trust in, there are ways to extend the shelf life of foods.

The following factors have a lot to do with extending shelf life: Storing bulk items in air-tight containers (bulk suppliers usually give the shelf life of their foods and offer recommendations for their optimal storage), the quality of the food when it was prepared for long-term storage, and whether food storage's worst enemies have been avoided: light, moisture, and extreme temperature (including temperature fluctuations).

Storing food at temperatures just above freezing vs. 70 degrees can quadruple the shelf life of bulk storage. Root cellars are excellent for storing bulk food storage as well as the overflow from the garden. If you have been considering a root cellar and want to build your own, websites with free DIY instructions have been added to the links at the end of this chapter.

Canned goods do not have the same storage needs as bulk foods. As long as you rotate your canned goods, using them before their shelf life has expired (typically two years), storing them at room temperature works fine. The rule of thumb for rotating your canned goods is first in, first out. Canned goods do not do well in moist, high humidity conditions, however, as this will cause the cans to rust. Any bulging cans must be tossed out. Do not store cans that are dented.

Be sure to date each can with an indelible marking pen. Stay organized. Store your canned goods in categories: fruits with fruits, vegetables with vegetables, and so on. Store new purchases of canned goods at the very back of your storage shelves with the oldest items in front within easy reach. Keep a clipboard with your food storage to jot down what was consumed and bring this list with you when you make trips to the grocery store to replace them. This method makes restocking shelves much easier.

# List of Suggested Suppliers and Reading Material

**Note:** Although the author has studied, and in some cases ordered from the following suggested sites, it is always wise to do your own research for the best pricing and availability for your geographic location. At the time of the publication of *Survival: Prepare Before Disaster Strikes,* each site listed was operational.

## Food Storage Shelf Life Chart

http://www.storeitfoods.com/shelf-life

http://survivalacres.com/information/shelflife.html

http://www.survivalmonkey.com/forum/general-survival/4123-shelf-life-food-storage-information.html

http://foodstoragemadeeasy.net/fsme/docs/shelflife.pdf

## Food Calculator

*Stock Up Foods Calculator; Very Detailed with (Have/Need) Inventory List*
http://www.stockupfood.com/members.php

*Container and Packaging Supply-Detailed Food Storage Calculator*
http://www.containerandpackaging.com/food_storage_calculator.asp

*About.Com Food Calculator*
http://lds.about.com/library/bl/faq/blcalculator.htm

Provident Living—Just the Basics Food Calculator
http://www.providentliving.org/content/display/0,11666,7498-1-4070-1,00.html

## Food Storage Buckets & Mylar Bag Suppliers

*Home Depot: Paint Buckets (Food Grade)*
http://www.homedepot.com/?cm_mmc=SEM|RPM|ST_Branded|BNG
_2897&skwcid=TC-14432-6068883085-e-634611514

*Big Tray Food Containers*
http://www.bigtray.com/catalog_3.asp?catid=13370&sr=gc&utm_sour
ce=google&utm_medium=cpc&utm_campaign=segments&utm_term=
food%20storage%20containers

*USA Emergency Supply*
https://www.usaemergencysupply.com/emergency_supplies/food_stora
ge_buckets.htm

## Emergency Supply: Storage Buckets & Mylar Bags

*Survival Solutions: Storage Buckets and Rotation Shelves*
http://www.survivalsolutions.com/store/Foodrotationshelves.html

*Disaster Stuff. Com—Storage Buckets and Much More Related to
Preparedness*
http://www.disasterstuff.com/store/pc/Food-Storage-Buckets-c12.htm

*Dry Pack Industries—Oxygen Absorbers*
http://www.drypak.com/oxygenAbsorbers.html?gclid=CMeSxpmn9aY
CFQqAgwod4yEpGg

*Honeyville Food Products—Oxygen Absorbers*
http://store.honeyvillegrain.com/oxygenabsorbers100cc.aspx

## Root Cellar/Cold Storage Pit/Pot-in-Pot Cooler/Refrigerator DIY

http://www.survival-spot.com/survival-blog/build-root-cellar/

*Basement Root Cellar*
http://www.organicgardening.com/learn-and-grow/building-root-cellar

*Video and Instructions for a DYI Root Cellar*
http://www.squidoo.com/build-your-own-underground-root-cellar-

# Chapter 7

# Avoiding Common Pitfalls

*"The sum of the whole matter is this, that our civilization
cannot survive materially unless it be redeemed spiritually."*
Woodrow Wilson

Food storage is new territory for many. This section is meant to help you avoid some of the more common mistakes that can sneak up and bite you on down the road.

## Don't Get Caught Short-Handed

People go about accumulating food storage in different ways. Many times food storage purchases are contingent upon cash flow and purchases are based on whatever is on sale. If you happen to find tuna fish for $0.50 per can, and your family likes tuna fish, stock up! Just be certain to search for the egg-free mayonnaise (that doesn't need refrigeration) or individual mayonnaise packets found at restaurant suppliers to go with it. Whenever a food item relies on another ingredient, be sure to add that item to the top of your list, so you will not be caught short-handed.

## Appetite Fatigue

Even in the midst of an emergency, children may not be as adaptable as you would like them to be. When forced to eat the same meal day after day, it is possible for children and some adults in your group to suffer Appetite Fatigue, a situation where they choose to go hungry.

As you build your food storage, be sure to add layers of tastes and textures. Comfort foods will help fight Appetite Fatigue. Put aside things your family already enjoys. For mine, it's pepperoni pizza and popcorn. Chef Boyardee has great off-the-shelf boxed pizza kits that come with packaged dough and canned sauce, including pepperoni. Being able to offer treats during a stressful time will make all the difference.

## Think Manually

As you begin putting food storage aside, jot down the manual appliances you will need and figure their costs into your budget. A 50-pound bucket of winter wheat may store for 30 years, but without a manual wheat grinder, its shelf life won't benefit anyone if the electrical grid crashes. It pains me to see how many online sites specializing in survival goods offer electric appliances. The least they could do is include a DISCLAIMER: *If you are certain that your area will not experience electrical outages, buy this product!* Why risk it?

Okay, if you had a pestle and mortar, you could grind it, albeit slowly, but it would take an immense amount of effort, and leave you no time for other necessary tasks. Remember, you are preparing for your and your loved ones' survival. It would be far better to purchase a reliable manual wheat grinder, or if money allows, purchase one with dual operations: both electric and manual.

At the heart of preparedness is the need to buy smart with as little guesswork as possible. Reflect upon how our forefathers lived, and conversely, those caught in Hurricane Katrina. Before industrialization, our forefathers relied heavily upon wood to cook and heat with. This approach was based upon sustainability and worked well for centuries. I never saw Lora Ingles shivering under blankets, trying to stay warm, nor do I recall Caroline Ingles running out of firewood to cook with. Think sustainable!

Very few caught in Katrina were prepared for the long haul and we all watched the devastating results on the news. So keep in mind: although electrical-run appliances are wonderful conveniences, the moment the electrical grid crashes, so can your ability to prepare food.

There is one exception to this rule. If you plan to sit out a crisis in a location that enjoys plenty of sunshine, solar panels or a solar generator are viable options and you *could* buy that electric wheat grinder. For the rest of us who live in northern climates, where the sun may not show itself for weeks at a time, the prudent thing to do is to purchase manual appliances.

## Practice, Practice, Practice

Take your food storage for a test drive; actually, many test drives. It will help your loved ones adjust to eating with storage foods and it will give you the practice to perfect mealtimes. In order to gain confidence, cook with your alternative cooking method. On paper, your preparations may seem like perfection itself, but when actually pressed into action, you may find your plan may need some tweaking.

## Silence is Golden, or Not...

As you begin preparing, it's natural to want to discuss your frustrations and successes with co-workers, friends, or neighbors. After all, why wouldn't you want to share that killer sale you got on packaged pancake mix, or the water purifier you finally found the money for?

In many ways, preparing for difficult times can be a lonely business. You may have cut back on luxuries like dinners out and have not seen the inside of your favorite store for far too long—if you did you would never be able to get prepared. You might even be having a tug-of-war concerning the costs of preparedness with those closest to you.

This can leave you feeling isolated, set aside from the rest of humanity, because you made the decision to be independent from a long line of desperate people when a crisis strikes. And you would not mind company on your journey.

Before you pour your heart out to anyone who is not included in your preparedness plan, give it some thought. Whoever you confide in *will* be beating a path to your door when a crisis strikes!

# List of Suggested Suppliers and Reading Material

**Note:** Although the author has studied, and in some cases ordered from the following suggested sites, it is always wise to do your own research for the best pricing and availability for your geographic location. At the time of the publication of *Survival: Prepare Before Disaster Strikes,* each site listed was operational.

**The Techniques of Food Storage
(Includes the Hazards of Appetite Fatigue)**

http://www.survival-center.com/foodfaq/ff3-grai.htm

*YouTube on Appetite Fatigue*
http://www.youtube.com/watch?v=b1OuBiRjt-8

# Chapter 8

# Repeat After Me:
# I Will Spend No More Than Necessary!

*"God places the heaviest burden on those who carry its weight."*
Reggie White.

Buying smart starts with deciding on the best food storage plan for your situation. Otherwise, you'll find yourself having to do expensive do-over's. Do your preferences lean towards lining your storage shelves with long shelf life foods and then forgetting about them until they are needed? If so, then MRE's, bulk, dehydrated, and freeze-dried foods are the best choice. Many foods packed in hermetically sealed #10 cans have a shelf life of 5 to 15 years. For wheat and white rice, the shelf life can be up to 30 years when packaged in airtight cans, and stored in a cool, dark, moisture-proof location.

If, on the other hand, you are on a tight budget or you gravitate more towards a hands-on sensibility, then canned goods might be the better choice. Most canned goods have a shelf life of 2 years or more (more on this later). This type of storage is managed with a "rotation method" as already mentioned.

## Planning Food Storage for Extended Family Members

When I first started out with food storage, there was no real "plan" at all, other than to fill my basement's storage shelves as quickly as possible. Looking back, it's clear I'd simply transferred my shop-till-you-drop mentality for creamed corn—bling in a can. Okay, it wasn't even a close second to designer anything, but at least I was doing something proactive. Eventually, it dawned on me that buying canned goods for one year for 22 people would mean I would need to purchase 2,300 lbs worth of canned fruit and 782 lbs of canned vegetables and on top of that was beef and chicken broth, and tomato sauces, and…well, you get the picture.

The biggest problem about having no real plan at all was that my children were grown and lived away from home. Continuing in this ill-advised direction, even if I'd holed myself up in my cabin and ate from morning 'till night, my canned food storage was going to see its shelf life come and go long before it could be consumed. Planning for canned goods as being the lion's share of food storage in such a circumstance is ill-advised. The only realistic approach when including a number of people who will be consuming food storage only when disaster strikes, is to buy long shelf life items and fill only a manageable portion of food storage shelves with convenient canned goods that can then be reasonably consumed and rotated.

## Overcoming Drawbacks: Dehydrated vs. Canned Goods

There are a few notable drawbacks with dehydrated vs. canned goods. Canned goods are packed in water, reducing the amount of water required for cooking. Canned food generally contains more fat, which in an emergency is beneficial to health when food reserves are limited. Finally, canned foods are approximately 25% cheaper than are dehydrated foods. Another challenge is a recent shortage of available dehydrated and freeze-dried foods. Therefore, it may take a bit of research to find a reliable source, so before placing an order verify the items you are ordering are available in a timely manner.

You can greatly reduce the cost of dehydrated foods by preparing them yourself. It requires a good book on the subject, however. There is an art to reducing the moisture content of fruits, vegetables, and meats in order to end up with successful long-term storage. Buying fruits and vegetables at the source, such as a pick-it-yourself farm or a farmers market, will save a bundle of money. Several do-it-yourself sites offering free instructions to build a solar dehydrator are supplied at the end of this chapter.

## Time Isn't Always on Our Side

Given enough time, having sufficient food storage is possible for each of us. But time isn't necessarily our friend in this regard. This chapter will help you save between 50% to 90% on food storage purchases by following a few simple tips which will get you up and running in as short a period of time as possible.

## Re-Thinking Purchasing Habits

I don't know about you, but clipping coupons was never my forte…until calculating how much it would cost to feed 22 people and comparing that with my bank account. My solution was to confine purchases to whatever was on sale. An Internet search brought me to an online grocery circular site. By the following day, a small section of my previously empty storage shelves held 100 cans of fruit. The savings was over one-half. Since then, trips to the grocery store have resulted in savings of up to 90%—all for a few minutes time. At the end of this chapter I have provided some of the more popular coupon sites, but it is by no means a complete list. I recommend that you do an online circular search for stores in your area and check them weekly for sales.

Most grocery stores hold annual or semi-annual "flat" sales on canned goods. Typically the savings is 50% of the original price. Check with your local grocery stores and find out when they hold their flat sales, and budget accordingly.

Even when purchasing dehydrated and freeze-dried foods, you can save money by doing a cost-comparison before purchasing. Be sure to check the shipping charges. In some cases, the "deal" you find can evaporate the minute you look at what they charge for shipping. One of my favorite suppliers, Honeyville Grains, charges a flat $5 fee for shipping, no matter how large your order is. A list of online bulk food providers is supplied at the end of this chapter.

Great savings can be found at grand openings. A northwest grocery chain opening in my area held a grand opening sale that advertised bulk oatmeal for $7.00 for 25 lb bags. I bought 300 pounds and saved $23 per bag, a total savings of $276 over the next cheapest price I had found.

Grocery wholesale stores, outlet stores, and Dollar Stores often sell for less. This is especially true for Dollar Stores with regards to their paper and cleaning products like toilet paper, paper plates, paper towels, bleach, laundry soap, dish soap, and hygiene products. As already mentioned, many Dollar Stores have recognized the need to carry more canned goods and have begun to beef up their food isles. Grocery outlet stores have great deals on their products, but it takes comparison shopping to get the best deal. More than once, when double-checking before a purchase, I discovered a local chain store was selling fruits or vegetables for 75% off—much cheaper than what could be found at the outlet stores.

For items like dry beans, cornmeal, rice, spaghetti, and macaroni, look to some of the bigger chain stores that sell in bulk. The results can cut your costs in more than half of what you would have paid for smaller bags of the same item. Note: health food stores and food co-ops, although convenient, tend to be more expensive. Do a cost comparison before purchasing. If GMO (Genetically Modified Foods) is a concern, it is important to ask before purchasing. Much of U.S. agriculture for wheat, soybean, and corn products is grown from GMO seed.

When you buy spices, buy smart, or they will eat up your budget in no time. The same grocery store chain advertising bags of oatmeal at such a killer deal happened to sell bulk spices. It didn't take long to realize a savings of 80% over traditionally packaged spices found on grocery store shelves. Bulk spices store well in canning jars. Just make sure to label them to take the guesswork out of your meal preparations. You can store them with your other bulk storage in a cool, dry, moisture-free location.

Before purchasing bulk items such as beans, wheat, or corn, check with your local growers. Craigslist brought me to a local wheat grower that sold hard red winter wheat for $0.29 a pound when every other source I had checked was charging $1.00 a pound or more. My goal was a mind-numbing 2,000 pounds (remember, I was providing for 22 people, and my goal was a year's worth of food storage). The savings for that wheat purchase alone was a whopping $1,400!

## Canned Meats Come with a High Price Tag

Items such as canned beef, chicken, pork, turkey, and ham will add another layer of texture and flavor to meals but they come with a higher price tag. For most of us, the answer lies with meat-flavored TVP (textured vegetable protein). Their shelf life is incredible, between 15 to 20 years when stored in hermetically sealed cans and they will provide meat-flavored protein and texture to meals at a modest price.

Seafood is another protein source you will want to consider, and when shopping carefully, they are much less expensive. A favorite outlet store here in the northwest often sells clams for $0.50 per can, and canned oysters for $0.60. Their shelf life is quite a bit shorter than is TVP (around 5 years). Still, they're great for providing variety to meals like oyster stew and clam linguini and are a welcome relief from beans and rice and soups so often a staple of food storage. Tuna fish can't be beat for its cost, and besides the obvious use for sandwiches, tuna fish will also add flavor and variety to pasta meals. Sardines are another great source of inexpensive protein. Because my storage plan includes some rotation, I have added many of these items to my storage shelves, but not so much that I can't keep on top of rotation and shelf life.

It's possible to save by canning your own meats if you have the canning supplies this requires. We've all noticed the cost of meat is increasing, but if you find a great sale, it's possible to save money by canning your own meats. Shelf life varies with home-canned foods, so be sure this method will work for your specific circumstances.

**Note**: Recently, the meltdown of the Fukushima nuclear plant in Japan has lead to valid concerns over the safety of seafood. Fish migrate, and over time, it is possible fish caught by U.S. commercial fishing fleets may be found to contain trace amounts of radiation. Always use due diligence when purchasing seafood.

## Plan Ahead for Convenience

As you start to list items for your food storage, include convenience foods. At the onset of a crisis, you will want to have easy-to-prepare meals like canned soups, chili, and stews on hand. They act as buffers, allowing you to prepare quick, no-fuss meals while gaining valuable time to kick your preparedness into gear. You should plan to have several days' worth of canned meals—at minimum—for when traditional cooking would be difficult at best.

## Beans & Rice

You have to start somewhere and dry beans and rice are an excellent jumping off point. Together, they are a perfect protein and are relatively inexpensive. I recommend getting started with the suggested amounts of beans and rice found at online food calculators. There are several sites listed at the end of this chapter. When purchasing beans, consider keeping a variety; great northern, lima, black turtle, red, kidney, pinto, navy, and split peas just to name a few.

**Note**: Beware of purchasing rice grown in Japan post the Fukushima nuclear meltdown. If labeling does not indicate a food's origin, pass. If your cooking fuel reserves will be minimal, it's best to purchase canned beans. Dry beans take up to two hours to cook—and sometimes longer—using quite a bit of fuel or wood, depending upon your cooking method. However, it's possible to shorten cooking time by using a pressure cooker. Be aware that black-eyed peas, lentils, and split peas cannot be cooked in pressure cookers.

# Bartering

Food staples are excellent bartering goods (more on this in Chapter 19, *Bartering for Survival*). During a crisis an item such as salt will be in high demand, and having extra put aside will allow you to barter with your neighbors for items you need. Actually, any one of the basic staples listed in Chapter 19 will be in high demand, but salt has a huge advantage. It has a shelf life of Methuselah and it's cheap!

# Nutrition and Storage Food's Shelf Life

Although you will want to research the shelf life of foods yourself, we might as well jump into the can of worms called the "recommended shelf life" of foods. I know...you don't need anything else thrown on your plate when you're already juggling water storage, food storage, alternate cooking and heating, and preparedness goods, but if I don't warn you, you're gonna hate me later.

The truth is, recommended food shelf life varies to ridiculous levels. Here's an example: When going to random sites for the recommended shelf life for a simple can of tuna, remember my advice of 5 years? My search gave me 5 different answers.

One little gem of 50 years was thrown into the ring by someone writing in response to an innocent question sent in by another member of a food blog. Poor baby. Should that advice be heeded, I perish the thought of what the outcome would be. I suspect the "expert" who supplied this answer was probably laughing into their morning coffee, wondering how many would bite. So, here comes rule #1. Never take the advice of a novice, and especially never heed the advice of a stranger on a blog or an advice site who has no real compulsion to fret over the safety of your food. Search for a site you know you can trust after carefully combing through the contents on their site. If my feet were held to the fire, I would suggest your visiting credible preparedness sites. They tend to share the methods they have used, many times for decades, and they have your best interest at heart. After all, most of these folks do not make a living off these sites; rather it is a labor of love. Lest you get 50-year shelf life advice for tuna fish, be careful about taking the advice from a fellow member on the site you go to unless they have had years of practical experience.

Now, back to the "expert" advice on the shelf life of tuna. Besides 50 years, my quick search brought results of 2 years, a nebulous 3-10 years, 4 years, and 5 years. It is true that most canned foods can be trusted (provided the can is not bulging or dented) for up to 6 months past the recommended shelf life posted on the can. All food producers are mandated to offer a "use by" date, and this date reflects the length of time the nutrients are optimal. Should a crisis arise, eating most canned goods past their prime is safe, within a prudent timeframe, it's just that the contents may not provide optimal nutrients.

One expert will tell you all-purpose flour has a shelf life of 6 months, and another advises 15 years. Some say brown rice will last 6 months, and others, 6 years. If you're new to food storage, this can be extremely frustrating and can make your food storage choices difficult.

So, besides seeking council from a site you trust, here's my advice after many years of prepping: Storage food is meant for surviving a crisis. Many experts, especially ones found at gourmet cooking sites, are coming from a Julia Child mindset, where flavor, texture, nutrition, and even color play a large part in their shelf life advice. Conversely, preparedness and survival sites are usually more concerned with survival and are not as militant about texture and color, and recognize that although nutrition is hugely important to survival, throwing out buckets of all-purpose flour that have been stored for 6 months is counterproductive. Let's face it, as long as food has not gone rancid, it's food, and for survival purposes, it will get you and your loved ones past a crisis.

There is another part of the equation with regards to a gourmet cook's advice vs. survival/preparedness advice. The gourmet cook assumes their audience stores their flour and rice in its original packaging in a pantry, cupboard, or an open shelf where it is exposed to air, sunlight, and temperature fluctuations. Under these conditions, advising a 6-month shelf life for brown rice and 6 months for all-purpose flour is legitimate. However, transferred to airtight, opaque containers and stored in a dark, cool, moisture-free environment, that same brown rice can be expected to have a much longer shelf life, and all purpose flour is even longer.

When making choices for storage foods, it is important to make nutritional comparisons while balancing it with a food's shelf life, but you should also consider whether or not your family is likely to eat it.

Let's use brown rice as an example. It is a fact that the nutritional value of brown rice is impressive. It contains B2, B3, B6, as well as manganese, selenium, magnesium, and fiber. Nutritionally, brown rice far exceeds the nutritional value of white rice. But, before stocking up on it, you should take into consideration that the natural oils in brown rice gives it a shorter shelf life than white rice.

Staying with our brown rice vs. white rice scenario, take into consideration what your family is used to eating. To use guerrilla tactics of purchasing only brown rice when your family pushes it around on their plates, or tries to feed it to the family dog during "normal" times may prove disastrous. Preference should serve as a buying sign for your food storage selections.

Another consideration is the cooking time of brown rice vs. white rice, for the difference is nearly double. If you have determined to use a camp stove and have limited propane, choosing foods that require less cooking time is important to survival.

The intention here is not to pummel the reputation of brown rice. Actually, many of us prefer it. But each of us has specific needs, life-styles, and eating preferences. A time of crisis is not the time to make drastic menu changes, because doing so can lead to a person choosing hunger (Appetite Fatigue) over eating something they dislike.

# List of Suggested Suppliers and Reading Material

**Note:** Although the author has studied, and in some cases ordered from the following suggested sites, it is always wise to do your own research for the best pricing and availability for your geographic location. At the time of the publication of *Survival: Prepare Before Disaster Strikes,* each site listed was operational.

## Grocery Circulars

http://www.ppgazette.com/circulars.php

http://www.safeway.com/IFL/Grocery/Weekly-Specials

http://www.sundaysaver.com

http://www.grocerycouponguide.com/articles/grocery-store-

## Coupon Links

http://www.mycoupons.com/

http://www.myultimatecouponbook.com/

http://coupons.smartsource.com

http://www.couponcabin.com

## Shelf Life Chart

*Blog: Daily Survival (great article and shelf life recommendations here)*
http://daily-survival.blogspot.com/2011/02/long-term-food-storage-shelf-life.html

*Survival Guide—has a wealth of food storage, preparedness and shelf life recommendations*
http://www.survival-center.com/guide/food.htm

*Compliments of General Survival Forum—very detailed/thorough*
http://www.survivalmonkey.com/forum/general-survival/4123-shelf-life-food-storage-information.html

*Captain Dave's is THE most self-sufficiency inclusive site on the net! Go to Table of Contents and prepared to be shocked!*
http://www.survival-center.com/foodfaq/ff18-shl.htm

## Food Rotation Articles/Blogs

*Excellent, detailed information on food rotation and much more!*
http://modernsurvivalblog.com/survival-kitchen/food-storage-and-food-rotation-challenges/

http://ldspreppers.com/entry.php/103-Food-Rotation-Shelves

## DIY Solar Food Dehydrator

http://ecobites.com/diy-recycling-projects/712?task=view

http://www.rootsimple.com/2008/10/build-solar-dehydrator.html

## Solar Dehydrator & Solar Oven kit Supplier

http://www.sunovenchef.com/solar-oven-cooking-food-dehydration-diy-solar-oven-dehydrator-kit/

## Bulk Food Providers

http://www.honeyvillegrain.com

http://www.bulkfoods.com

http://www.bulkwholefoods.com

http://www.aaoobfoods.com/bulkfoods.htm

*Also Suppliers of Canned Butter*
http://www.pleasanthillgrain.com

# Chapter 9

# Okay! Break Open the Piggybank...

*"If you want to know what God thinks of money,
just look at the people He gave it to."*
Dorothy Parker

Now it's finally time to put your knowledge to work and start filling those lonely storage shelves, or closets, or wherever your imagination has lead you to safely store your food.

The list provided in this chapter is basic, meant to get you started with a budget in mind. If you have the cash flow to forge ahead, do so by all means. It's a fact that a variety of meals, textures, and flavors will make food storage much more palatable. On the other hand, you may feel compelled to put aside as many of the basics as possible, so that should a calamity strike, you will be prepared for the long-term. In the end, several things will lead you to your comfort zone: cash flow, food preference, and intuition. It is my honest belief that if you trust your instincts with regard to timelines, you will not be let down.

Your first purchase might be one or more cookbooks written specifically for cooking with food storage. As each of us have unique food preferences and cooking requirements, I suggest researching cookbooks that make the most sense for you and your loved ones.

You will find a wealth of free information at preparedness/survival blogs and web sites that graciously share their favorite home storage recipes. Print the recipes you like and keep them in a 3-ring binder for safekeeping. It is important to print your recipes to avoid the disappointment of trying to access them from your computer when the power grid has failed. With practice, you will become confident with the subtle difference of cooking with home storage. Once you have the hang of it, you might even try adjusting your favorite recipes for use with home storage cooking. The familiarity of eating "normal" food will be a great comfort, especially during a protracted crisis.

Make sure to jot down the ingredients and spices you will need for the new recipes you find. By keeping this list handy, you can refer to it whenever you go shopping and purchase whatever is on sale.

The list provided in this chapter is subjective and meant to provide protein, texture, and flavor to various dishes based on bulk staples such as beans and rice. For the most part, the list includes less expensive foods to get you started. You'll notice the list also provides for baked goods such as cornbread, biscuits, and occasional treats like cakes and muffins. You will want to adjust the list to your specific dietary needs and add your favorite foods to your list. Ultimately, no one knows your loved ones better than you do. If your child refuses a specific food, it matters little if every survival book you read suggests it for food storage. Find a replacement, or double up on something else they *will* eat.

**Note:** At the end of the supplied storage food list specific information is provided for items that have been highlighted.

## The Basics

| | |
|---|---|
| *Wheat | *Powdered Butter/Margarine |
| Flour | Corn Meal |
| Granulated Sugar | Oatmeal |
| Brown Sugar | Honey |
| Powdered Sugar | Jam/Jelly |
| Powdered Eggs | Peanut Butter |
| Powdered Milk | Rice |
| Evaporated Milk | Pancake Mix |

# Spices

Assorted Spices, depending on preferences and recipe needs

| | |
|---|---|
| Beef Bullion | Onion Powder |
| Chicken Bullion | Pepper |
| Garlic Powder | Salt |

# Baking Supplies

| | |
|---|---|
| Baking Powder | *Crisco or Other Shortening |
| Baking Soda | Maple Extract |
| Cocoa Powder | Molasses |
| *Cooking Oil | Vanilla Extract |
| Corn Starch | *Yeast |
| Corn Syrup | |

# Cooking Supplies

| | |
|---|---|
| Beef Broth | Tomato Paste |
| Chicken Broth | Stewed Tomatoes |
| Worchester Sauce | Vinegar |
| Tomato Sauce | |

# Pasta

| | |
|---|---|
| Spaghetti Noodles | Linguini |
| Fettuccini | Macaroni |

# Canned & Dry Beans and Legumes

| | |
|---|---|
| Kidney | Lentils |
| Great Northern | Lima |
| Split Pea | Pinto |
| Black Turtle | |

## Canned Meat & Seafood

Beef Chunks
Ham
Spam
Tuna Fish
Salmon

Oysters
Clams
Real Bacon Bits
TVP-Meat Flavored

## Condiments

Catsup/Ketchup
Mayonnaise/Salad Spread
Mustard
Salad Dressing, Bottled or Dry

Soy Sauce
Syrup
Worchester Sauce

## Convenience Meals

Boxed Pizza Kits
Canned Chili
Canned Pork & Beans
Canned Stew
Macaroni and Cheese

Soups-Assorted
Spaghetti-O's
Spaghetti Sauce
Top Ramen

## Fruit: Canned & Dehydrated

Applesauce
Apricots
Berries-Assorted
Fruit Cocktail
Grapefruit

Peaches
Pears
Pineapple
Plums
Prunes

## Vegetables: Canned & Dehydrated

Carrots
Corn
Green Beans
Peas

Potato
Mixed Vegetables
Spinach

## Comfort Food

Boxed Pudding
Boxed Jell-O
Brownie Mixes
Cake Mixes
Canned Nuts
Chocolate Chips

Cookie Mix
Fruit Rollups
Hard Candy
Popcorn
Trail Mix

## Special Needs

Baby Food

Baby Formula

## General Information

### Storing Flour

Flour is the most basic of staples and it would be hard to imagine getting along without it. But before you decide on whether to store wheat flour or white flour, realize they have different shelf lives. White flour can be stored for up to 18 months or longer, whereas wheat flour has a shelf life of approximately 6 months. The reason for this is wheat flour has natural oils that turn wheat flour rancid more quickly. If you have the room, you can store wheat flour in a freezer to extend its shelf life.

### Bulk Whole Wheat

Whole Hard Wheat is a good choice for storage food because it has a shelf life of thirty years when stored correctly.

There are several types of wheat with hard white wheat and hard red wheat being the most popular. Both have gluten and protein to give elasticity and strength to bread dough, but red wheat can be more difficult for the body to digest; something to keep in mind when cooking for small children and the elderly.

Another difference is their taste. Hard red wheat gives breads a hearty, strong wheat flavor, while hard white wheat has a lighter flavor. Either variety has more vitamins and fiber than does processed flour.

Whole Soft Wheat is typically used for baking cookies, cakes, pastry, piecrusts, and biscuits because it yields a much lighter baked product than does hard wheat. It is lower in protein and gluten, but still offers more nutrition than processed flour.

Durum Wheat is perfect for making pastas, as it is the hardest of the wheat family. It is sometimes referred to as semolina.

* Even when water is limited, wheat can be sprouted to provide fresh greens.

* Combining wheat and heirloom garden seed offers a reliable, sustainable way of life. If you decide to store wheat, it is important to purchase a manual wheat grinder. Prices vary greatly, but for a real powerhouse that will grind your wheat with ease, look into a Country Living Wheat Mill ™. They cost around $400, but they can't be beat. Other manufacturers sell manual wheat grinders for $40 on up. Be sure to purchase replacement parts for whatever model you chose.

* If you are interested in making your own pastas, there are many affordable manually operated pasta makers on the market.

**Note:** Hard wheat can be purchased from local growers at a fraction of the cost of online bulk food suppliers.

### Sourdough Starter

It is wise to keep a favorite sourdough starter recipe on hand for a protracted crisis. Yeast has a disappointing shelf life of 6 months to two years, depending upon the type and the way it is stored. For a dependable way to bake bread, sourdough starter can be kept unrefrigerated. Just be sure to print the recipe!

Take time to practice baking with sourdough starter, so when the time comes when you need it, you'll be a pro! Besides, if your family and friends are giving you sideways looks about all the food storage piling up on your basement shelves, you will have the opportunity to show them your wisdom, and how yummy food storage can be.

Recipes for sourdough starter are provided in Chapter 17, *What's for Dinner?*

## You Should Know

**Butter and margarine** is available dehydrated in #10 cans, found at online and at retail survival/preparedness suppliers. Butter can also be purchased tinned. Because of the expense, many people just starting food storage opt to add it later, when preparations are complete and money for more expensive items is freed up.

**Cooking oil** has a short shelf life of up to one year. Once opened, its shelf life is between a few weeks to a few months, depending upon what type of oil you are purchasing and whether preservatives have been added. This is problematic as young children and the elderly need the extra calories cooking oil provides to avoid weight loss. Purchasing cooking oil in smaller containers and storing them in a cool, dark location will help lessen the problem of shelf life. If you have the space, you can store cooking oil in your refrigerator to extend its shelf life.

**Butter flavored Crisco** or a similar butter flavored shortening is a good substitute for baking that calls for butter or margarine. It has a shelf life of 8 to 10 years.

**Eggs** can be purchased in powdered form in #10 cans and can be used for baking once re-constituted. If your budget doesn't allow for this addition to your storage, you can preserve farm-fresh eggs. Instructions on preserving eggs is found in Chapter 17, *What's for Dinner?*

**Jams & Jellies:** Once a jar of jam or jelly has been opened, it does not need to be refrigerated. Typically, they will last for over a week on your pantry shelf as long as you take care to use clean utensils each time you use it. If you are uncertain if you would consume even a small container of jam or jelly in the course of one week, individual packets of jams and jelly's can be found online at restaurant suppliers.

I have also seen them at Costco on occasion.

**Mayonnaise**, we all know, is kept refrigerated. You may have read advice from globetrotting boaters who swear they've never gotten sick from non-refrigerated mayonnaise. They simply caution to use a clean utensil when using it to avoid contamination. I'd like to believe them, but have to admit to being terrified of testing this theory during a crisis when food poisoning is not an option. Consider squeezable-container Miracle Whip spread or another sandwich spread that does not contain egg product and that does not require refrigeration. Another option is to purchase individual packets of Mayonnaise through online restaurant supply companies. Costco sometimes carries boxed 200-count individual mayonnaise packets.

**Cake yeast** has a short shelf life of 6 months vs. dry yeast with a shelf life of up to 2 years—5 years when refrigerated. An alternative is using sourdough starter. For general information on sourdough starter, refer to Chapter 17, *What's for Dinner?*

# List of Suggested Suppliers and Reading Material

**Note:** Although the author has studied, and in some cases ordered from the following suggested sites, it is always wise to do your own research for the best pricing and availability for your geographic location. At the time of the publication of *Survival: Prepare Before Disaster Strikes,* each site listed was operational.

### Freeze-Dried/TVP/MRE's

http://wisefoodchoice.com/?gclid=COOdyv2Z0qkCFRE3gwodu As8hA

http://www.nitro-pak.com/products/freeze-dried-foods

http://www.mredepot.com/servlet/StoreFront

http://www.ineed2prepare.com

http://www.foodinsurance.com

http://www.beprepared.com

http://survivalacres.com/information/shelflife.html

http://www.foodstorageprepare.com

http://www.pleasanthillgrain.com/

http://preparedplanet.com

### Bulk Food Providers

http://www.honeyvillegrain.com

http://www.bulkfoods.com

http://www.bulkwholefoods.com

http://www.aaoobfoods.com/bulkfoods.htm

*Also suppliers of canned butter*
http://www.pleasanthillgrain.com

## Restaurant Suppliers

*Individual jam, mayonnaise and more*
http://www.webstaurantstore.com/85/condiment-pc-packets.html

# Chapter 10

# Layering Food Storage

*"God gives every bird its food, but he does not throw it in its nest."*
J.G. Holland

Layering food storage allows you to get creative and turn basic survival food up a notch for meals you look forward to cooking and eating.

You will notice that this list is predominately made up of bulk and dehydrated food items. As already discussed, dehydrated fruits and vegetables tend to be more expensive and that's why they are suggested *after* basic food storage has been put aside. None of the suggested food staples found in Chapter 9, *Okay! Break Open Your Piggybanks...* have been included here, other than in bulk form, so if you are still gathering basics, remember to include anything still missing on your list to the one below.


## Layering

Almonds
Cake Mix, Bulk
Carrots, Dehydrated
Cherries, Dehydrated or Canned
Chocolate Chips, Bulk or Packaged
Chocolate Syrup
Celery, Dehydrated
Cheese, Powdered or Canned Cheese Sauce
Cookie Mix, Bulk
Corn, Bulk or Dehydrated

Cornmeal, Bulk
Frosting, Assorted, Containerized or Dry
Fruit Drinks, Bulk or Packaged
Green Beans, Dehydrated
Hot Chocolate Mix
Jalapeno Peppers, Dehydrated or Canned
Macaroni, Bulk
Milk, Dehydrated, Bulk or Canned
Muffin Mix, Assorted, Bulk, Dry or Boxed
Mushrooms, Dehydrated or Canned
Noodles (Assorted), Bulk
Onions, Dehydrated
Peaches, Dehydrated
Pears, Dehydrated
Potato, Dehydrated, Bulk-Cubed/Sliced/Wedges/Flakes
Potato, Instant, or #10 Cans
Peas, Dehydrated
Popcorn, Bulk
Soup Mixes, Bulk, Dry
Soup Stock, Bulk, Dry
Strawberries, Dehydrated
Tomato, Powdered
Tomato, Sun Dried
Strawberries, Freeze-Dried
Vegetables (Mixed), Dehydrated
Walnuts

## Meats and Seafood...Yes!

Items such as canned beef, chicken, pork, turkey, and seafood will add another layer to the variety you are able to serve when cooking with bulk storage. It's amazing what you can find canned.

Some of the items, such as canned bacon and beef products are costly and are sometimes difficult to find, with the exception of specialty online stores. To cut costs, try places like Costco and Wal-Mart and other large chain stores before turning to online suppliers. I've noticed just recently that Fred Meyers, a local superstore chain in the northwest, has begun to carry canned beef. If you are on a budget, you might want to add the more expensive canned meats at the end of your food storage preparations when cash flow is freed up. There are creative workarounds you might want to consider such as replacing canned bacon with bottled real bacon bits. They will add flavor to meals at a fraction of the cost. Another solution is to can your own meats. Basic canning information is available in Chapter 14, *Root Cellars & Home Canning*.

## Meats & Seafood

| | |
|---|---|
| Bacon, Canned | Pork |
| Bacon Bits, Bottled | Pot Roast |
| Chicken | Salmon |
| Clams | Sardines |
| Clams, Smoked | Shrimp |
| Corned Beef | Spam |
| Crab | Steak |
| Hamburger | Stew Meat |
| Oysters | Turkey |
| Oysters, Smoked | |

## The Spice Cabinet

Keeping a variety of spices and condiments on hand will add variety to the flavor of meals, no matter how basic your food storage is.

The following are spices found in many food storage recipes. As you build your food storage and begin to collect recipes online and in cookbooks, your personal list may vary. When a spice is called for in a recipe that is beyond your budget, exchange it for something similar, or omit it altogether. It is doubtful anyone will notice if a pinch of saffron or cardamom is missing from a recipe.

**Note**: Remember to research before you buy. Many grocery stores sell bulk spices for a fraction of the cost of what you will pay for fancy packaged spices lining the grocer's shelf.

## Spices and Baking Extracts

Allspice

Almond Extract

Alum

Basil

Beef Bullion

Caraway

Cardamom

Cayenne

Celery Seed

Chicken Bullion

Chili Powder

Chili Seasoning Mix, Dry

Chives

Cinnamon

Coriander

Cloves

Cumin

Curry

Dill

Garlic Powder

Ginger

Kitchen Bouquet, Bottled

Lemon Extract

Lemon Pepper

Liquid Smoke, Bottled

Mace

Marjoram

Mint

Mustard, Dry

Nutmeg

Onion Powder

Oregano

Paprika

Parsley

Peppermint Extract

Pickles

Poppy Seeds

Rosemary

Saffron

Sage

Savory

Sesame Seed

Taco Seasoning Mix, Dry

Tarragon

Thyme

Turmeric

## Condiments

Barbeque Sauce

Chili Sauce

Relish

Salsa

Steak Sauce

Tabasco

# List of Suggested Suppliers and Reading Material

**Note:** Although the author has studied, and in some cases ordered from the following suggested sites, it is always wise to do your own research for the best pricing and availability for your geographic location. At the time of the publication of *Survival: Prepare Before Disaster Strikes,* each site listed was operational.

## Bulk Food Providers

http://www.honeyvillegrain.com

http://waltonfeed.com/

http://www.bulkfoods.com

http://www.bulkwholefoods.com/

http://www.aaoobfoods.com/bulkfoods.htm

*Also suppliers of canned butter*
http://www.pleasanthillgrain.com

## Freeze Dried & TVP

http://wisefoodchoice.com/?gclid=COOdyv2Z0qkCFRE3gwodu
As8hA

http://www.mredepot.com/servlet/StoreFront

http://www.nitro-pak.com/

http://www.ineed2prepare.com/

http://www.foodinsurance.com/

http://www.beprepared.com/

http://survivalacres.com/information/shelflife.html

http://www.foodstorageprepare.com/

http://www.pleasanthillgrain.com/
http://www.readyreservefoods.com/
http://www.survival-warehouse.com/
http://preparedplanet.com

## Canned Meats, Cheese & Butter

http://www.mredepot.com/servlet/StoreFront
http://www.aaoobfoods.com/cannedmeats.htm
http://www.readydepot.com/servlet/Categories
http://www.campingsurvival.com/camechbu.html

# Chapter 11

# Survival Goods

*"It is not necessary to change. Survival is not mandatory."*
W. Edwards Deming

If you haven't visited a hardware or a camping store recently, it's time to hit the pavement and shop for the survival goods that will see you through a crisis. As you will notice as you review the list, food storage alone is not enough to see you through a protracted crisis. Please, don't let the suggested list overwhelm you, for not everything listed will pertain to your preparedness plan. It would make no sense to go out and buy plywood for an outhouse if you happen to live in a ten-story condo. On the other hand, if you live in a rural setting, having the materials set aside to build an outhouse for when the power goes down, will make everyday life much more bearable.

Everyday items such as plates and silverware are not listed with the following survival goods list, so if your idea of dinner is reservations, you will want to add these items to your personal list. A separate list for gardening, animal care, and home canning is provided in their respective chapters.

## An Heir and a Spare

It's important to duplicate essential items such as can openers. To have something so basic fail in the midst of a crisis would not be a good thing. Think "an heir and a spare" with regards to critical goods.

## When to Break the Rules

Although depending upon tools, cookware, and appliances that depend upon electricity, gasoline, or propane is not recommended for basic survival, a few exceptions have been included in the survival goods list. These super convenient items are best purchased after purchasing priority foods and preparedness goods and you've caught the addictive self-reliance bug and want to keep going. An item like a chainsaw is admittedly a luxury when a reliable axe or two-man saw will suffice. But some rules beg to be broken. If you have the money, having a chainsaw for replenishing your firewood would be manna from heaven. So would a 4-wheeler for transportation. Just be sure to put aside fuel for these items, and if you plan to store large quantities for any length of time, look into fuel extenders.

**Note:** Storing fuel in 55-gallon drums below ground and covered with a piece of plywood serves two purposes: it is safer and will hide them from view.

## Entertainment

If you have children in your household, your preparedness may hardly register a blip on the screen when a crisis strikes. They *will* notice when they run out of coloring crayons or craft items that would keep them otherwise occupied! For this reason, an activities list of basic supplies has been included. Recipes for making finger paints and Play Dough can be found at the end of Chapter 17, *What's for Dinner?*

## Stocking up on Prescription Medicines

If you take daily prescription medicines you should have a talk with your doctor about extra prescriptions. In the event your doctor is unable to supply the supplemental prescription (doctors are highly regulated with regards to writing prescriptions nowadays), you should investigate a naturopathic alternative. Some "preppers" have turned to online ordering, but beware if you go this route. Lately there have been warnings that prescriptions ordered overseas are not always what they promise.

# Preparedness Goods

## <u>Activities</u>

Board Games
Books
Coloring Books
Colored Marking Pens
Crayons
Colored Pencils
Dice
Finger Paints
Hobby Items

Notebooks
Paper
Pens & Pencils
Play Dough
Playing Cards
Outdoor Games: Horseshoes,
    Badminton, Volleyball,
    Tetherball, Lawn Croquet

## <u>Camping Gear</u>

Anti-Gravity Water Pump
Axe
Back Pack
Batteries
Canteens
Coffee Pot, Camp or
   Percolator Style
Coleman Style Lanterns
Compass
Cooking Utensils
Dutch Oven
Eating Utensils
Fire Pit Tripod
First Aid Kit
Flashlight, both Battery
   and Shake Style
Flint Fire Starter
Folding Chair

Hatchet
Head Lamp
Hunting Knife
Maps
Matches, Waterproof
Mess Kit
Nylon Rope
Shovel, Folding
Sleeping Matt
Solar Lanterns
Swiss Army Knife
Tarps
Tent
Two-Way Radios
Water Bottle
Water Canteen
Water Containers, Collapsible
Water Purifier, Camp Sized

## Cooking Implements

Bread Pans
Can Opener(s)
Cooking Thermometer
Cast Iron Dutch Oven
Cast Iron Pots & Pans
Coffee Maker, Camp
    Style Percolator

Egg Beater, Manual
Egg Timer
Heavy Oven Mitts
Measuring Cup(s)
Meat Grinder, Manual
Reflector Oven

## Cleaning Products

Bleach*
Dish Soap
Laundry Soap, Liquid

Scrubbing Pads
Scrubbing Powder

* Even if your budget is tight, try to put aside extra containers of Bleach for bartering. It's inexpensive and will be in great demand in a crisis.

## Clothing

Boots
Coats, Especially Warm
    Coats for Winter
Gloves
Hats
Hiking Boots
Kerchiefs

Long Johns
Mittens
Rain Poncho
Scarves
Socks, Cotton and Wool
Tennis Shoes
Underwear

## Communications

Ham Radio
Two-Way radios
Wind-Up Emergency Radio

Battery-Run Radio
Solar Radio

## Fuel Source

Firewood
Gasoline
Kerosene

Lamp Oil
Propane
Other Camp Stove Fuels

## Hygiene Products

Body Lotion
Body Soap
Cotton Balls
Cream Rinse
Dental Floss
Deodorant

Diapers
Feminine Products
Shampoo
Tampons
Toothpaste
Toothbrush

## Larger Goods & Appliances

Burning Barrel
Chainsaw
Firewood
Generator, Solar or
    Gasoline-run
Hand Cart
Hand Dolly

Propane Canisters
Sheppard's Stove
Water Purifier
Wringer Washer
Wood Cook Stove
Two-Man Tree Felling Saw
Tree-Felling Axe

## Lighting

Candles
Head Lamp
Hurricane Lamp
Lantern Mantles
Oil Lamp

Kerosene Lamp
Flashlights, Battery-run, Solar
    and Shake Style
Wall Lamp Hangers
Replacement Wicks

## Medicines & Medical Supplies

Ace Bandage
Adhesive Pads
Antacids

Aspirin
Athletes Foot Cream
Athletes Foot Powder

Baby Powder
Bandages
Birth Control
Books on Medical
    Emergencies, First Aid,
    and Dental Repair
Butterfly Clips
Cold & Flu Medicines
Children's Tylenol
Children's Cold & Flu
    Medicine
Children's Thermometer
Calamine
Dental Kit
Diaper Rash Ointment
Eye Wash
Epson Salts
Gauze
Gauze Pads

Gauze Roll
Ice Pack
Iodine Solution
Kaopectate
Ibuprofen
Hot Water Bottle
Hydrogen Peroxide
Latex Gloves
Isopropyl (Rubbing Alcohol)
Neosporin
Pepto Bismol
Surgical Tape
Sunscreen
Suture Kit
Oral Thermometer
Toothache Medicine
Vaseline
Vitamins, Various

## Miscellaneous Household Goods

Ash Pail
Batteries
Bungee Cords, Various Sizes
Candles
Clothes Pegs
Duct Tape
Fireplace Grate
Fireplace Set

Heavy-Mill Plastic, To Cover
    Windows and Doors and
    Misc. Use
Map, Local and Topographical
Nylon Rope, Various Sizes
    and Lengths
Pails, Various Sizes
Twine
Tubs, Various Sizes
Washtub

## Paper & Storage Products

Aluminum Foil
Paper Plates

Paper Towels
Plastic Cups

Plastic Garbage Bags,
Various Sizes
Plastic Wrap
Storage Food Keepers

with Lids
Toilet Paper
Water Storage Containers
Zip Lock Bags, Various Sizes

## Tools & Building Materials

Automotive Tools and
Replacement Parts
Allen Wrench
Bolts
Chicken Wire
Flat Head Screwdriver
Hammer
Heavy-Mill Plastic,
Blackout and Clear
Monkey Wrench

Nails, Assorted Sizes
Nuts
Phillips Head Screwdriver
Plywood
Saw
Screws, Assorted Sizes
2 X 4's
4 X 6's
Washers

# Chapter 12

# Shelter:
# More Than Just a Roof Over Your Head

*"I had rather be on my farm than be emperor of the world."*
George Washington

Most of us are entrenched in our lifestyles, our surroundings, and our jobs. To uproot our lives for a cabin in the woods might appear to be a departure from sanity. It might also appear to be financially impossible, even if you could get past the idea of such an abrupt lifestyle change. You could be one of many who are financially upside down in their homes, or you might have concerns over finding employment in a more rural area. Basically, there are as many valid reasons to remain where you are as there are people on this spinning globe we call earth.

It boils down to priorities and opportunity. Recognizing that you are the only one who understands your unique circumstances, I invite you to think about your situation and open yourself up to the possibilities. The reason I ask this is the same one that led me to write this book. I am promoting self-sufficiency at a time when climate change threatens our safety, terrorism looms menacingly over our heads, and the promises we have been given about America's solvency conflicts with every aspect of life as we know it.

### It can't hurt to throw out a few possibilities, so here goes...

You don't have to go it alone. Family and friends may be thinking in terms of self-sufficiency as well, and you'll never know unless you ask them. Pooling money and skills can get you off-grid and independent much sooner than trying to go it alone. Money is a good thing to have lying around when contemplating a cabin in the woods, but if you have nothing in the bank, your hard work and skills can be just as bankable—the time is money principle. If you are efficient at home canning, gardening, studding out walls, hanging drywall, nailing shingles on a roof, or if you can hunt and fish or have medical experience, your talents will be golden during a crisis. Sit down and brainstorm with those you trust and see what you come up with. You might be pleasantly surprised!

There is strength in numbers and even if we lived to the ripe old age of 90, and studied self-sufficiency daily, practicing every conceivable survival principle, we would never attain the skills to call ourselves an expert on everything. So, not only does it make financial sense to ban together with those we trust, it makes practical sense as well.

If you live in a city and own a home or condo, consider taking a leap of faith and sell it or rent it out for a move to a more rural setting. With land to grow a sustainable garden and a water well, your self-sufficiency potential just rose into the stratosphere! It is possible to find a cabin or a manufactured home for rent if your pocketbook can't take the strain of a purchase.

If you have a job in the city, you could investigate the possibility of working from home, and that home could be off-grid. If not, there are still moneymakers that only require a desk and a computer. Perhaps you've thought about selling on eBay, or Amazon. If so, you could always take your idea for a test drive before pulling the plug. You might also want to look in to beekeeping, fish farms, worm farms, or raising goats and chickens for profit.

Think about your skills and what you enjoy doing most. Does it carry with it the potential for independent living?

The following information about purchasing or building a cabin doesn't necessarily involve the perfect homestead, for we don't live in a perfect world. The just-getting-by cabin will work wonders for self-sufficiency.

## The Lower the Profile, the Better

The more basic a homestead appears to passersby, the better. If your cabin in the woods happens to be a 3,000 square-foot showpiece with a glass-fronted prow, thrill seekers industrious enough to snag the gas to get to your neck of the woods *will* take notice. And based on what they see from the outside, they will probably decide your getaway is ripe for the pickin's: generator, chainsaw, 4-wheeler, with plenty of food storage and survival goods. Unfortunately, they would probably be right! So think minimalist, or have plenty of backup to protect what's yours.

Conversely, if funds are tight, a cabin can be built on skids for all it matters. If it has room enough to store food, and enough floor or attic space to sleep your group, then it'll be a palace when disaster strikes.

## Rural Property & Circumventing Land Mines of Owner-Finance

Most of us have dreams of buying a cabin or a home on acreage, but if you haven't been able to afford your dream property, take heart. There may be factors you are unaware of.

Get Your Land For Free! Yes, you heard right! Recently, struggling communities have begun to offer plots of land for free. If you are not shy of open spaces with few amenities, and you are willing to pre-qualify for a home loan, or build within a certain timeframe, it's time to do an Internet search to see what's available.

It's likely this trend will continue as small towns seek to draw new blood. What's the catch? With each new resident, these struggling communities receive increased revenue from the government for schools. They also stand to gain property and income tax revenues.

But keep in mind the value should be in the property, not the improvement if you wish to cushion yourself against plummeting real estate values. If you have your heart set on a specific location, and a modern day run to the open plains doesn't pique your interest, there are great deals on both developed and undeveloped properties out there these days, provided you keep in mind the lion's share of investment should be in the property. Historically, acreage does not have a tendency to "crash" as does brick and mortar.

When friends or family ask for advice about purchasing a home in the city or a suburb in today's market, I advise against it. There is a good chance the market will continue to adjust lower than current levels. Having said that, investing in land where you can raise farm animals and grow a garden is not the same as buying a McMansion. Property that allows you to provide for the future is a lifestyle choice that offers the ability to survive whatever the economy has in mind for us in the future.

## Where to Find the Best Deals on Rural Property

For Sale by Owner properties are often more affordable, provided the seller lowers the price of their property by the 6% to 7% normally paid to a real estate agent. Just make sure that you do your homework when dealing with a For Sale by Owner, so the savings you realize by leaving out a professional won't come back to bite you later on (more on this later).

Lease Purchase is on the increase and for those concerned over where the real estate market is headed, this approach is safest. Typically, you will pay the same first month, last month, and damage deposit as you would with a rental, only in this case a portion of the monthly "rent" goes towards your down payment. The benefit of a lease-purchase is that you can live the lifestyle you choose, but should the market take a nosedive, the price can be renegotiated before purchase. Have a professional look over the paperwork of a lease purchase before committing to it.

Raw Land is an option for a handyman who has the skills to build their own cabin or for those who plan to have their dwelling professionally built. While living in Alaska, it was common to meet homesteaders who dug basements and lived there while they built up cash and carry. Others started with a garage or small barn and utilized the space as home base while they built their home as money became available.

There are innovative ways to build DIY nowadays, including straw bale, cordwood, and cob. If you are handy and don't mind lots of hard work, you can save an incredible amount of money by building your own home. Another approach is a modular home. They haven't suffered the same prejudice as manufactured homes have with lenders, and rural home loans are still available for modular homes. They are drop-shipped to your building site and with help, they can be erected in a reasonable amount of time.

One of the biggest upfront costs and risks of buying raw land is drilling a well. It helps to have a perk test done on the property, which should be provided by the seller. My advice is to negotiate to have the seller pay to have a well dug and roll the costs back into the property sales contract. It takes out the guesswork.

Mortgages have never been available on raw, unimproved land, as mortgage lenders attach the improvement (home or cabin), rather than the land, should a borrower default. Before the recent real estate crash, owners often held out for a cash sale on raw land, but those days are long gone, leaving sellers open to owner-carry contracts. When negotiating the interest rate on a loan, keep in mind that the interest rate you pay the seller will be far better than the banks are paying for interest accrued on monies sitting in an account. There is always room for negotiation!

Owner-carry loans are not the same as a lease purchase. They are binding sales contracts agreed by the buyer and seller at a specific interest rate for a specified period of time. As the buyer of a property, the interest rate on an owner-carry contract can be written off at income tax time.

It's possible to find screaming deals on owner-carry loans, but go into this type of real estate loan with your eyes wide open. Most of the time, you will be dealing with an honest owner who simply needs to get out from under a property. Rural settings come with greater difficulties with regard to mortgage loans and many times lead to sub-prime loans (with higher interest rates), but as mortgage lenders grow increasingly wary of what they deem as risk, these types of loans have all but dried up. Sellers aware of this are moving towards the owner-carry loan when they own the property outright.

As with any business deal, there is the potential for predatory practices involving real estate that may have you headed for court. Should a seller ask for interest rates that steadily climb over time, or request a balloon payment, beware! There will be more on this later under *Watch Out for Red Flags!*

Multi-family homes have made up a sizeable portion of home sales over the past few years. Groups of families have banded together to help one another through this shaky time, and I for one applaud them. Gardening and homesteading chores can be shared, and by pooling resources, financial solvency is much more likely.

Mortgage loans for group ownership are fairly simple to do with a Tenancy In Common—but be aware that not all states allow them. When seeking such a loan, it is best to refer to an attorney to address issues such as how taxes and property improvements will be divided. It is also important to agree on inheritance issues should a member pass away.

Thinking outside the box may lead to interesting alternatives. If you have a pioneering spirit, what about pulling a fifth wheel trailer onto an undeveloped property and living in it while you build your home? By selling the fifth wheel once your structure is complete, you stand to recoup the money spent on your temporary shelter. Many have done this with great financial results!

Manufactured homes have always been a financing challenge, and have been hit hard with the current real estate downswing. Where once sub-prime loans were available for manufactured homes, they are now difficult to find, as mortgage lenders grow increasingly squeamish to risk.

For the most part, manufactured homes are located in rural settings due to building codes that disallow them in many towns, cities and some suburbs; therefore great deals can be had on them in today's market. Sellers who have paid off their mortgages and need to sell have turned to owner financing and in some cases the asking price may be pennies on the dollar.

Before you search, however, be aware that in the U.S. manufactured homes older than June 15, 1976, were not eligible for financing even during the real estate boom and certainly will not be in the future. The problem is poor snow loads built into roof structures and issues with insufficient insulation. Even for those who can afford to pay cash, keep in mind, should you decide to sell your property later on, you may have a difficult time finding someone willing to hand over a chunk of cash.

Other concerns to watch for are manufactured homes that have been moved more than once or a singlewide. A manufactured home that has been moved from, say, a park to a property is disqualified from a mortgage loan.

The problem that surrounds a singlewide is their history of depreciation, of which lenders are only all too aware. Loans on singlewide manufactured homes are difficult to find, and when found, always come with a high interest rate.

The exception to the rule is purchasing a property that comes with a giveaway trailer or manufactured home—usually dilapidated or older than June 15, 1976. This strategy works well for anyone interested in building a home or cabin and needs a roof over their head in the meantime. Be aware that once you are finished building your home, it costs upwards of $1,000 or more to move a trailer or manufactured home from the property, depending on roads and the distance involved.

## Watch Out for Red Flags!

Earnest money agreements should always include rights of refusal should the property not pass a home inspection or title search. Be certain to include other contingencies such as loan approval. This will ensure that your earnest money deposit is refunded to you if your financing falls through. In a case where you must sell an existing home, the earnest money agreement should include a clause stating that if you are not able to sell your home within the timeframe you and the seller agree on (typically 60 to 90 days), your earnest money deposit will be reimbursed in full.

Owners cannot be expected to watch out for your interests and they are not held to the standards of professional real estate agents. Always watch out for your own interests!

The amount of an earnest money down payment is negotiable, and many times, a deposit of $1,000 is sufficient to prove your interest, but no more.

Seek a professional if you are unclear about an owner finance, lease purchase, or lease option property agreement, because once you've signed, it becomes a legally binding contract.

Title insurance is relatively inexpensive for the protection it offers a buyer and should be part of a sales agreement, even when it isn't mandatory to a sales contract. Title insurance protects you against builder's liens, property tax and income tax liens, building code issues (like discovering the shed that came with the property is built partially on your neighbor's land and must be moved) and it will verify that the seller is the legal owner of the property with the right to enter into the sales contract. They also verify that your property is not in a floodplain, something to be avoided, as not only is your property at greater risk, but floodplain insurance is usually ten times the annual expense of a normal homeowner's policy.

Set up an escrow account so that payments you make each month have a third party involved to verify that the payments were made. That way, should a dispute arise, you have solid proof of payment history. Escrow payments can usually be set up to pay homeowner's insurance and property tax along with the mortgage payment each month, which avoids the annual surprise when the full bill comes due.

Home inspections should always be performed, even when you are paying cash or the property is owner financed—especially when it is owner financing. It's doubtful an owner would offer you a checklist of everything wrong with a home. To find out the substructure of your new cabin is termite-ridden or the foundation is on the verge of collapse after a purchase means untold headaches and legal battles down the road.

Should a problem be revealed that could be repaired by you, this is a perfect opportunity to take the amount of repair and labor off the sales price. With hard work, you'll be able to build instant equity in your new property.

Don't overpay, especially in a market that hovers up and down and plummets without warning. Offering 10% to 20% less on a property helps protect your investment. This is not a case of taking advantage of the seller, but rather cushioning your investment against the threat of market decline.

Request the owner of the property pay for an appraisal to ensure you pay no more than a property is worth. If you can't get the owner's agreement, you should consider paying for the appraisal yourself. Traditional loans require an appraisal. Owner carry does not. Practice due diligence!

However, if money is tight, there is another way to determine market value of a property through title companies. Most have programs they can run in your specific area to help you determine valuation. Assessment departments in the area may also be able to help. When all else fails, you can approach a real estate agent and trade their expertise for a modest gift certificate to their favorite restaurant.

Credit rating doesn't always compute with homeowner finance. It's not uncommon for the transaction to be done without a credit check. For many, short-term financial hiccups lead to dings in credit rating, but in this case, the seller is more concerned with the down payment made to their property. The larger the down payment, the less likely it is that you will default on the loan. Buyer default returns ownership of a property to the seller. Any improvements made to the property, monthly payments, and your down payment remain with the original owner and they are free to resell the property to someone else. For this reason, it is wise to negotiate a cushion of time before the default process takes effect, which can be written into the sales contract. Should you lose a job or suffer a temporary setback, you will have the advantage of extra time to recover.

Balloon payments can be a death knell to a property owner when they come due! For instance, should you agree to a balloon payment 5 years from the original property sale agreement, you must either secure a loan or pay cash to the owner by the date agreed upon. Considering rural home loans are getting harder to find, and there is no way of knowing what the state of the market will be at that 5-year mark, you stand the chance of losing the property if you are unable to find a loan or produce cash. This would put you in default and any improvements, payments and down payment is retained by the seller, leaving them free to resell the property.

Don't agree to sliding interest rates as many times they are a "hook" to reel in buyers. It is easy to get distracted by that "perfect" property and ignore the ramifications of a sliding interest rate that steadily climbs. This practice makes it easy to pay the property payments at the beginning of the contract, but may force you to refinance soon after, or lose the property

"Grand-fathered" properties are properties built before new building codes and thus excused from new regulations until changes are made. Therefore, should you find that jewel of a cabin overlooking the lake as perfect once a second story is added, better look before you leap!

Should you attempt to do an addition on a grand-fathered property, you may find that your jewel of a cabin just became a noose around your neck.

## Must-Haves

If you have already purchased your cabin, or are planning to build a cabin, there are a few improvements you can plan for that will make your life a lot easier. Providing storage in a cool, dark space is optimal. But if storage space is minimal, and you have the time and a little extra cash, think about a root cellar. They're great for storing some of your bulk food and any overflow from a garden. Free plans can be found on the Internet for do-it-yourselfers. Links are provided at the end of this chapter. Instructional books on building a root cellar are available. If you are on a budget, search for used ones on Amazon.

Plan for a manual hand pump for your well. Water is just as important as food. The other must-have is a wood stove or a wood cook stove for cooking and heating. As discussed in Chapter 5, many newer model wood burning cook stoves can be purchased with water reservoirs.

If the only improvement you can make to your homestead is storage space, a manual hand pump and a wood burning cook stove, then you've done well.

If your building plans or cabin do not include a bathroom, then look at it as a blessing—building an outhouse will get you prepared for off-grid living that much faster. If you have plans to dig a well, refer to the end of Chapter 3, Water Sources, Purification, and Storage for Fred Dungan's step-by-step instructions, *Do-It-Yourself Water Well.*

# List of Suggested Suppliers and Reading Material

**Note:** Although the author has studied, and in some cases ordered from the following suggested sites, it is always wise to do your own research for the best pricing and availability for your geographic location. At the time of the publication of *Survival: Prepare Before Disaster Strikes,* each site listed was operational.

## Do-It-Yourself Outhouse Building Plans

*Outhouse DIY and information on other modes of waste management*
http://www.i4at.org/lib2/hmnwaste.htm

http://cottagelife.com/14313/diy/projects/perfect-privy-3

*Thorough instructions, with pictures, on building an outhouse*
http://www.checkthisshitout.com/2009/05/building-an-outhouse/

## Do-It-Yourself Shed Building Plans

http://buildingashed.org/

*YouTube "How to build a shed" and offers free plans*
http://www.youtube.com/watch?v=zXUAI0FqPdQ

## DIY Root Cellar

http://www.survival-spot.com/survival-blog/build-root-cellar/

*Made from Pallets*
http://theepicenter.com/tow1102.html

# Chapter 13

# Gardening Starts From the Ground Up

*"Earth is so kind, that just tickle her with a hoe
and she laughs with a harvest."*
Douglass William Jerrold

To write only one chapter about gardening and calling it good is a
lot like diving off a high dive into a child's wading pool: impossible! However, gardening is specific to climate zones and individual
needs such as containerized gardening for those living in urban settings.

If you are new to gardening, you should invest in an in-depth gardening book that spells out the how-to's of successful soil preparation,
composting, and what fruits and vegetables grow best in your climate
zone. This is the reason why there are so many books written on the
subject and why they have a tendency to fly off the bookshelves. You
will want to get at least one all-inclusive book on gardening, and preferably several. There are gardening books on seed starting, on starting
early plants in the home or a greenhouse, square foot and containerized gardening for city living, and gardening books specifically written for climatic zones.

For anyone already gardening, know that we aren't alone. The National Gardening Association reports that some 43 million U.S. households are growing their own vegetables, fruits and herbs, an increase
of 7 million, up 19 percent. An estimated 21% are first-time gardeners.
When polled as to why they had turned to gardening, they report an
interest in providing healthy food for the table and the need to recession-proof their lives. Smart folks! Nothing was mentioned about the

type of seed being used, but I'd like to believe most bought heirloom seed so their efforts lead to lush gardens and seed that can be saved from one growing season to the next.

To be successful with gardening means educating yourself on the typical pests found in your specific climate zone. If your area is prone to a specific aphid or slug, for instance, having the means to rid your garden of them could mean the difference between eating and going hungry.

Gardening is a buffer against troubled times, whether they were brought on by a job loss, a national crisis, or disruptions in the food chain. Gardening is sustainable. When everything else is falling down around us, the good earth and a few seeds can help make things right, offering us bounty. To handle the overflow of such bounty, home canning is a good solution, and the reason why home canning basics are discussed in Chapter 14, *Root Cellars & Home Canning.*

## All Seed is Not Created Equally

Why the multi-national seed suppliers would hire scientists to cross-engineer seed, playing God with our food supply defies explanation, but that's exactly what's happened. GMO seed is outlawed in many countries because of health concerns over eating food from this seed when there has not been proper testing. Already, several court cases have led to a moratorium on GMO seed, but due to the clout these mega-corporations have, the restrictions were lifted and we were once again turned into host monkeys. Genetically altered foods make up more and more of our food supply and judging from lab studies on rats and amphibians, the news doesn't look good. To date, low birth rates, infertility, auto-immune disease, allergies, and gastro-intestinal illness have been reported with controlled studies.

If we want to be assured of self-sufficiency by growing healthy food, we need to turn to the wisdom of our forefathers. They grew from heirloom seed that was viewed as nothing less than a means for survival. Today, things haven't changed all that much and heirloom seed is viewed by folks involved with preparedness as an inexpensive insurance plan for a time when bulk, canned, or MRE food storage gives out during a long-term crisis.

Heirloom seed is also referred to as non-hybrid, or open pollinated seed. Do your homework before you decide which supplier to order from by investigating what seed is provided in their packaged deal, if that's the way you will be ordering (it's possible to order individual heirloom seed). Seed is not one size fits all and you will want to make sure the seed the supplier ships to you will grow well in your climate zone.

## It Starts With the Good Earth

You can't plant a garden without exposed earth. Most garden plants need six hours of direct sunlight each day, so when deciding on where to clear land for a garden, bear this in mind. Keep watch over the area you've designated for your garden. Does it meet the sunlight requirement? If so, get started by clearing away any undergrowth and avoid tilling wild grasses or lawn into your soil!

## When All Else Fails, Make a Lasagna Garden

If the job of clearing out undergrowth seems overwhelming, make a lasagna garden instead. The name brings visions of growing the ingredients for a vegetarian lasagna, but in truth a lasagna garden is a method of layering a designated garden area with newspaper or cardboard and then alternating layers of materials that condition the garden area into a rich loom without the need to dig out sod or weeds. Here is how it's done:

The first layer of your lasagna garden starts with a layer of brown corrugated cardboard or several layers of newspaper placed directly on top of the grass and weeds of your designated spot. Soak it down and decomposition will start doing its thing by smothering the vegetation beneath it.

This next step might bring out the kid in you—if your inner child ever left to begin with. Think of it as an out of control combination art and cooking class which starts with throwing on your first "ingredient" or "color" from the list provided below. If you use manure (brown), then the next layer should be green, which for the lasagna garden could be lawn clippings, weeds, and kitchen fruit and vegetable scraps. The only rule of thumb is to make your brown layers about twice as deep as your green layers, but just as with cooking or art, it isn't such an exact science that the fun and spontaneity needs to be removed from the mix altogether. Your goal is to end up with a two-foot layered bed.

## Browns

| | |
|---|---|
| Manure | Peat Moss |
| Compost | Shredded Newspaper |
| Fall Leaves | Topsoil |
| Coffee Grounds | Newspaper |
| Tea Leaves and Tea Bags | Peat |

## Greens

| | |
|---|---|
| Grass Clippings | Pine Needles |
| Fruit and Vegetable | Garden Trimmings |
| Table Scraps | |

You can start a lasagna garden whenever you'd like, but because Fall provides abundant leaves and yard clippings, it makes your work a bit easier to start a lasagna garden in the Fall.

## Test Your Soil

Gardening experts advise waiting six months before planting a garden after amending garden soil, so it's best not to put off testing your garden soil.

There are two types of tests that will allow you to check the condition of garden soil: ones you can buy cheaply at a garden center or a big-box hardware store, and others where you have the soil professionally tested. Going the professional route is more expensive, unless you have a local county or university extension office nearby. Many times, they perform soil tests inexpensively.

It's never a good idea to simply take the advice of a neighbor who's had success with gardening. It's possible over the years they have added compost and mulch and nutrients to their garden soil, and the quality between their garden soil and yours may be wildly different.

What you're testing for is the pH level of your garden soil. If you use one of the do-it-yourself kits, they provide directions on how to read the test results and offer advice on remediating your soil for optimal growing results.

The pH level of soil will have a reading of between 1 to 14. Anything higher than a 7 means your soil is low in acidity, and anything below a 7 means your soil has higher acidity. The results need to be taken to heart, and the soil should be adjusted accordingly, because the slightest wavering from "optimal" will have an impact on the yield of garden production. For instance, a reading of 6 is 10 times more acidic than a 7 (7 being a neutral reading).

Another factor to consider is whether you're on well or city water. Deep wells are often more alkaline and watering garden plants with it will lower a garden soil's acidity. To find out about your well or city water's pH level requires having your water tested.

## Earthworms

Earthworms benefit the garden by tunneling into the earth, opening up the soil, and exposing it to the air. This tunneling enriches the soil with nutrients for the lush garden plants we desire, and it helps with irrigation as we water our plants. Their travel through the soil leaves room for the delicate root system of plants to branch out, offering them better absorption for nutrients and moisture. Not only that, but the worm's waste product contributes phosphorus, potassium and nitrogen to the soil that greatly benefits the health of vegetables and other garden plants.

It may be hard to view the common earthworm as the pit bull of the garden, but in many ways they are! Earthworm waste product acts as a natural repellant for garden pests and it helps to protect garden soil from disease.

To make a worm farm, all you need is a container, shredded newspaper, soil and worms. Here's how you make one:

Scrounge or purchase a bin around 2 feet X 3 feet that's at least 12 inches high. Make a "nest" of shredded paper to approximately 8 to 10 inches high. Mix in 1 to 1 ½ pounds of rich garden soil. The final step to make their house a "home" is to add water to moisten, not soak, the contents, and mix the shredded paper and the soil together. Before introducing your worms to their new home, let the moistened soil and shredded paper sit for 48 hours to meld.

Worms thrive in temperatures of between 60 to 90 degrees. Any hotter or colder may have you tossing out their poor little corpses, so heed the temperature of where you place them!

If you are someone who enjoys digging, you can collect your own earthworms, or you can go online and order them.


## Composting

If you've ever marveled over the rich soil found in the garden of a diehard gardener, chances are they have added compost to their soil. Introducing compost that has been allowed to evolve into rich humus in with garden soil costs nothing and the rewards are great. Humus releases minerals and nutrients such as nitrogen, phosphorus, potassium, iron, iodide, copper, zinc, cobalt, manganese, and molybdenum into the soil—dependent upon what goes into your compost. Humus also negates the need for fertilizer, as humus *is* fertilizer, but it is fertilizer in its most pure, organic state.

So what should you feed your compost pile? Well, the good news is much of what is delivered to the local landfill can be re-directed to the compost pile. Compost can contain kitchen waste, yard clippings, leaves, weeds, and even paper products. Other than the occasional paper product, the rule to follow is "living" things. However, avoid dairy and meat products, as this will attract vermin. Plant materials such as weeds and grass will decay quickly, so to avoid turning compost into a stinky heap, mix in an equal portion of kitchen scraps as well as leaves and wood products which tend to decompose slowly. Tree limbs and other heavier wood products should be reduced in size through shedding or chopping first before adding them to compost or they will not decompose correctly.

Compost is not finicky and enjoys coffee grounds and old tealeaves. Starbucks got on the bandwagon of organic gardening toot sweet, offering their composting patrons free coffee grounds. If you live close to a busy coffee shop, give them a try.

If you happen to have cows, goats, sheep, horses, or chickens, their manure gets along quite well with compost and will add another layer of richness to the dark, rich, sweet-smelling humus your compost will produce. And feel free to toss in the used straw left over from the chicken coop.

For purists, compost can be kept in a pile and protected from the elements by covering it with plastic sheeting or cardboard. It can also be kept in a decorative bin with solid sides and a lid. If your compost bin is made with slats, exposing compost, line it with straw. Either way, just remember to feed your compost often, stirring it every once in a while to let the decomposing materials "meld". Just as with garden soil, compost is benefited when you let earthworms work their miracles. As the earthworms tunnel through your compost bin, feasting on food scraps and organic waste, they open up the compost materials to the air and that, in turn, promotes moisture which turbo-charges the materials in your compost into rich humus. Here too, their waste product enriches your compost with nutrients, improving the environment of your vegetable garden. If you decide to buy earthworms through the Internet, look specifically for the best "workers" such as Red Wigglers or Red Earthworms under the search terms vermiculture, vermicompost, vermicast, worm hummus, worm manure, worm castings, or worm composting.

## Mulch

No matter what growing zone you live in, mulch is an important component to gardening. Mulch captures moisture, thus reducing watering requirements. At a time when every drop of water counts, it will be your new best friend.

## Would You Like a Little Water with That Plant?

Gardening books do not typically mention planning for a time when the water spigot runs dry—namely it's grid-down and the water district is out of power. If you have a well, you can pre-plan a diversion to your garden area with a hand pump. Anyone dependent upon the water district will want to research an affordable water containment system, which is discussed in Chapter 3.

## Plan for a Greenhouse

I know, adding one more thing to the list isn't fair. But when you think of the garden as a lifeline—and it is—then planning for a simple greenhouse is a reasonable project to add to the to-do list.

A greenhouse will protect your fruits and vegetables from weather extremes. Although none of us can know what Mother Nature has planned for us, we can look to the weather anomalies recently experienced across the globe, and take a pretty good guess. Depending upon your expertise with a hammer and nails, you might be interested in going to the U.S. Department of Agriculture for their free software download for greenhouse plans found under "Virtual Grower" to build your own greenhouse. You might also want to search bookstores and the Internet for greenhouse building ideas and instructions.

Kits are available that vary in price and quality, so do your homework before purchasing. Buying a pre-built greenhouse may seem the easiest route at first blush, but the delivery costs may be hard on the pocketbook.

Before you purchase, consider an attached greenhouse that benefits from the warmth of your home and offers the convenience of easier access.

If your finances are already stretched, a very basic greenhouse can be put together with heavy-mill plastic and 2 X 4's, although a windstorm might wreak havoc with it, so set aside extra materials just in case.

Whichever direction you decide to go, the minimum size recommended by experts is 8 by 10 feet. If your greenhouse plans are merely to start seedlings a bit earlier in the spring, an unheated greenhouse can give you an extra twelve weeks of growing time.

If your plans are for year-round gardening for optimal food output, consider a larger greenhouse. If you live in a colder climate zone, a small wood burning device like a potbelly stove will keep plants happy.

## Deer Have No Table Manners

Deer would just as soon use your garden for mealtime and leave their droppings in exchange. It takes an 8 to 10 foot fence to keep deer out of a garden due to their incredible jumping ability. T-Post fencing is an inexpensive solution.

Some experts recommend a shorter fence with electric fencing on top to jolt, not kill, the deer. But, if the grid goes down, they'll be right back at your lettuce. Others swear by attaching shiny metal pie plates attached to a pole. This setup allows the pie plate to move in the wind and its reflective surface supposedly frightens the deer.

After researching all of the possibilities you might decide on a solar "electric" fence, as it doesn't draw all that much power, which means it won't hurt the deer, but it *will* improve their garden manners. Solar fencing is independent of the grid, fairly inexpensive, dependable and easy to install.

## Bad Bugs

It isn't just deer that will eat your food. The list is long and not only includes animals, but critters who glide in on wings, and others that slither in. When you get your all-inclusive garden book, look for the common offenders for your climate zone and jot down what you will need to keep them from devouring your garden.

## Most Common Bugs Found in the Garden

**Aphids** feed on nearly all garden plants and transmit disease and viruses. They cluster on unopened flower buds and the underside of leaves and are found on the stems of plants. Be on the lookout for leaves that take on a wilted appearance—especially with regards to the leaves of tomatoes and watermelon plants. Aphids are prolific, so you'll want to check your garden regularly for this pest, or they can take over a garden. Aphids come in all sizes, shapes and colors.

**Cabbage Loopers** are common and feed on many plants, most notably cabbage, collards, cauliflower and broccoli. As caterpillars, they are smooth and green with white stripes. The adult moths are brown with silver or white figure eights on their wings. They are attracted to older leaves. To double check plants for the Cabbage Looper, turn over the leaves of older plants and if found, pick them off.

**Cutworms** are caterpillars that are gray, black or brown in color that tuck into a tight curl when disturbed. They live in the soil and come out at night. They'll chew on any plant but can do untold damage to tomatoes, cutting tomato transplants off at the soil surface.

**Earwigs** can cause serious damage to flowers, vegetables, fruits and other plants. Keep an eye out for them in your garden and look for leaves that have a ragged appearance with small, irregular holes.

**Grasshoppers** are voracious eaters and will happily decimate the foliage of a garden in no time if left alone. They are partial to corn, beans, peppers, peas, broccoli and squash. They are the biggest threat to a garden when they are traveling in swarms. Organic bait containing *Nosema locustae* can be used to kill grasshoppers.

**Leaf-footed Bugs** are identified by the wide spot on each hind leg that resembles a small leaf. They suck the sap from plants. Fruit crops are their favorite, but they will also feast on vegetable plants. When young, they are small and red or orange in color with black legs. The only known organic control for the Leaf-footed Bug is hand picking.

**Leaf Hoppers** attack mostly leafy vegetables like potatoes, spinach, lettuce and sometimes carrot tops. Signs that your garden has the Leaf Hopper are yellowing stunted growth and twisted leaves of the lettuce plant.

**Spotted Cucumber Beetles** look a lot like a green ladybug and are very detrimental to the garden. They carry the virus *Bacterial Wilt* that can attack vine vegetables, and once infected, there is no cure.

**Striped Blister Beetles** (also called Army Beetle) come in swarms and can lay waste to any type of vegetable, but particularly tomatoes, squash, beans, melons, and peppers. Conversely, their larva is beneficial to the garden, as they feed upon grasshopper eggs. An organic method to kill the Striped Blister Beetle is to sprinkle flour on them, which gums the wings and legs and eventually kills them.

**Tomato Hornworms** are large green caterpillars, which when adults, are the Five-Spotted Hawk Moth. They will ravenously eat the foliage of tomatoes, peppers, eggplants and potatoes, and are capable of stripping a tomato plant of its foliage nearly overnight. The best treatment for tomato hornworms is to watch for them and destroy them when found.

These are just a few of the harmful insects found in the garden. The best way to control harmful pests is to learn to identify them, know what signs to look for, and to do regular checks for them in your garden.

## Good Bugs

**Tachinid Flies** resemble houseflies but live outdoors where they eat garden pests like tent caterpillars, gypsy moth larvae, and cutworms.

**Braconid Wasps** like to feed on caterpillars and sawfly larvae. Braconid Wasps are beneficial to tomatoes, as one of their favorite foods is hornworm that can decimate tomato plants in little more than a day.

**Bumblebees** visit dandelion, rhododendron blossom, foxglove, and rosebushes, collecting nectar and pollinating fruit and vegetable plants.

**Earthworms** are mentioned here because though they may not be a bug or seek and destroy harmful insects, they are certainly efficient composters and offer rich nutrients to your garden plants. They're not happy in clay based or sandy soils, so encourage them to live in your garden by enriching your garden soil with compost.

**Green Lacewings** prefers a meal of soft-bodied garden pests, including aphids, thrips, red mites, small caterpillars, and mealy bugs that feed on the foliage of plants.

**Ground Beetles** enjoy eating slugs, snails, cutworms, and root maggots.

**Ladybugs** are partial to soft-bodied aphids, mites, and mealy bugs.

**Nematodes** are microscopic parasites that live in the soil. White grubs, flea larvae and Japanese beetles are all susceptible to nematodes.

**Praying Mantis** is a "mixed bag" insect as they don't discriminate between beneficial insects from bad. However, it consumes mosquitoes, nocturnal moths, bees, beetles, small lizards, and frogs. They are cannibalistic and include other praying mantises in their meal plan.

**Spined Soldier Bugs,** also referred to as "stink bugs" because of the foul odor they emit when disturbed make a meal of Mexican bean beetles, Colorado potato beetles, hornworms, cabbage loopers, and cabbage worms.

## Encourage Beneficial Bugs in Your Garden

Avoid using insecticides. Insecticides cannot discriminate between the good bugs and the bad bugs and they contain chemicals you don't want to introduce into your garden.

Do grow plants that will attract beneficial bugs like clover, cosmos, hostas, marigolds, sage and sunflowers.

## Natural Weed Control Methods

**Vinegar:** This method is dependant on the weather, as you will need 3 to 4 rain-free days for the use of vinegar treatment to be effective. Sunlight will do the rest. Fill a spray bottle with full strength white vinegar. Spray the leaves, stem and around the base of weeds, being careful not to over spray onto your plants. Because vinegar will leach into the ground, it's best to pull the weeds close to your garden plants instead of using vinegar.

**Corn Gluten Meal** is a weed control method that will stop weeds from germinating, but it won't kill existing weeds. It works by dehydrating the weed seeds as they attempt to sprout. Corn gluten meal will not harm your garden plants. In fact, it is a good source of nitrogen

**Boiling Water:** Take the boiling water out to your garden, preferably in a teapot or kettle. Pour the hot water directly on the weed. This will kill the weed all the way to the root.

**Dishwashing Soap and Water:** Mix five parts water to one part soap in a spray bottle or a container. Pour or spray mixture on the weeds.

**Alcohol and Water:** A few tablespoons of rubbing alcohol in a quart of water is all it takes. You can use a spray bottle or a container to apply to the weeds.

**Rock Salt:** Sprinkle rock salt around the base of weeds. Within in a few days, they'll be dead.

**The Old Fashioned Way:** There's always the shovel. Just make sure you dig down deep enough to get the root, or the weed *will* be returning.

## Create a Habitat to Attract Pollinators

Over the past several years there have been a large number of honeybee die-offs reported by beekeepers that eventually became known as Colony Collapse Disorder. Speculation on the causes of Colony Collapse Disorder ranges from nicotine-based pesticides to cell phone towers and electrical interference. Studies have found evidence of parasitic mites and antibiotic-resistant pathogens in affected hives. Whatever the cause, Colony Collapse Disorder has led to the die-off of over half of many beekeepers' hives. Considering that 35 percent of our food crops depend upon pollination, this collapse disorder could have a huge impact on the food chain.

If you want to ensure that fruits and vegetables such as tomatoes are pollinated, either plan to hand pollinate (the link is provided at the end of this chapter), or make a habitat-friendly environment for pollinators. The requirements aren't that great. What you'll need is a garden site or a containerized garden in a location that receives six hours of sunlight each day. If you want to attract a variety of pollinators, be sure to plant a variety of plant types such as trees, shrubs, perennials, annual flowers and herbs. Different pollinators have different needs during their lifecycle stages and this is covered below.

Because the pollinators in a specific region will naturally be drawn to native plants, research what grows in your area. Consider heirloom varieties that provide easy access to nectar and pollen; in some cases hybrid adaptations may not be as user-friendly for a pollinator.

What flowers you will want to plant for a pollinator garden depends upon what you are trying to entice to your garden.

**Bats** that pollinate are found primarily in the Southwest. Their preferences are large, light-colored, night-blooming flowers with a strong fruity odor like that found in cacti.

**Bees** like yellow, blue and purple flowers. Even though bees can't see the color red, they are still attracted to bee balm because of its ultraviolet properties. Smaller bees tend to be attracted to daisy, butterfly weed, and aromatic herbs.

**Beetles** are happiest with open flowers like aster, sunflower, rose, and butterfly weed.

**Butterflies** are attracted to red, orange, yellow, pink and blue flowers. They prefer flat-topped clusters found in zinnia, calendula, butterfly weed, yarrow and daisy that are planted in a sunny location. The food sources they need for developing larvae are milkweed, aster, lupine, thistle, fennel, violets, hollyhock, and black-eyed Susan.

**Flies** are drawn to green, white, or cream colored flowers with simple bowl shapes.

**Hummingbirds** are attracted to red, orange, purple and red tubular flowers that provide plenty of nectar. The best candidates are honeysuckle, sage, fuchsia, jewelweed, fireweed, cardinal flower, bee balm, nasturtium and the century plant.

**Moths** prefer light-colored flowers that open at night like the evening primrose.

It is important to plan for flowers to bloom throughout the year, so a constant food source is available. Planting trees and shrubs such as dogwood, blueberry, cherry, plum and willow will provide nectar or pollen in early spring when other food sources are scarce.

Provide plants with leafy vegetation to accommodate larval stages of the butterfly and other pollinators. Wild grasses, Milkweed and Queen Anne's Lace work well.

As with every living thing, pollinators need water. Butterflies enjoy "puddling", where they congregate to drink. A muddy puddle makes them happy, or you can fill a pan with damp sand and set it in your habitat garden. A birdbath can provide water for birds and other pollinators. Bees need water to build hives while other pollinators require the minerals found in ground water and mud.

As your pollinator garden takes shape, you can add creative touches that serve a dual purpose by providing nesting materials for pollinators like upside down flowerpots with holes in the bottom, twigs, straw, and possibly a bird house or two. The point is to encourage pollinators to stay and make themselves at home.

## Basic Garden Tools

The following is a basic list of garden tools you'll need to have on hand for a backyard garden. The list will naturally be shorter for containerized gardening. Garden tools come in different lengths and for the most part, the longer-handled tools will make working in a large garden easier. Always keep extra handles on hand for repairs. If you're on a tight budget, look for these tools at garage sales, craigslist, and thrift stores.

## Must-Have Garden Tools

Garden Spading Fork, used for soil turning, aeration and mixing materials like compost

Garden/Digging Spade, used for digging, and also for edging

Garden Hoe, they are available in many different styles and are used mainly for weeding

Garden Rake, used for leveling the soil and clearing out debris

Garden Sheers, used for cutting dead leaves and branches

Hori-Hori Knife, used for digging, weeding and planting

Garden Pruners

Garden Gloves

Garden Stakes

Shovel

Trowel

Twine

Wheelbarrow

# List of Suggested Suppliers and Reading Material

**Note:** Although the author has studied, and in some cases ordered from the following suggested sites, it is always wise to do your own research for the best pricing and availability for your geographic location. At the time of the publication of *Survival: Prepare Before Disaster Strikes,* each site listed was operational.

### Hand Pollination How-To

http://www.ehow.com/how_2102682_hand-pollinate-garden-plants.html

### Informative Garden Sites/Blogs

http://www.family-survival-planning.com/vegetable-gardening-tips.html

http://www.suite101.com/content/abasicvegetablegarden-a59

http://mygrandpasgarden.com/home////blog1.php?disp=comments

http://www.homefarming.com/Category/1

http://inmykitchengarden.blogspot.com/

http://ncmg.blogspot.com/

### Greenhouse Information

*Informational Site About Greenhouses—Read up on the difference between Heirloom, Hybrid and GMO Seed*
http://www.greenhouses.net/

http://karenshanley.com/blog/2008/01/whats-the-difference-between-heirloom-hybrid-and-gmo-seeds/

http://organic.lovetoknow.com/Non_GMO_Seeds

## Know the Dangers of GMO Seed

http://www.livestrong.com/article/216714-dangers-of-gmo-foods/

http://www.responsibletechnology.org/gmo-dangers

## Do-It-Yourself Greenhouses

*DIY Step-by-Step PVC Greenhouse*
http://pvcgreenhouse.blogspot.com/

*Free Greenhouse Plan*
http://www.floridagardener.com/greenhouse/greenhousematerials.htm

*How to Build a Hoop House*
http://www.diynetwork.com/how-to/how-to-build-a-hoop-house/index.html

# Chapter 14

# Root Cellars & Home Canning

*"Don't let the fear of the time it will take to accomplish something
stand in the way of your doing it. The time will pass anyway;
we might just as well put that passing time to the best possible use."*
Earl Nightingale

It's unfortunate that preparedness isn't one-stop-shopping. But preparedness is a lot like remodeling a home. You might start with the kitchen counters, upgrading them to granite. Once they're installed, suddenly the floor looks its age next to the shiny new countertops, and the walls need a bit of help, and what about the sink?

As you delve deeper into preparedness and set aside a spot for your garden, it will eventually become clear you'll need a way to store the garden's overflow—a great problem to have, actually, but one that needs to be addressed. Root cellars are a great place to start, for when done right, they can store your garden's bounty through the winter. Home canning and dehydration are other solutions to store the overflow from the garden. Most folks involved with preparedness for any length of time typically combine several food storage methods.

## Root Cellars: Mother Nature's Refrigerator

The use of root cellars goes as far back as 17th century England. In the United States root cellars are back in vogue as people look for sustainable lifestyles and need a solution to store a garden's bounty. A root cellar's benefits don't stop with preserving fruits and vegetables. When built correctly, they can perform double-duty as a fallout shelter.

Traditionally, root cellars are dug into a hillside or a slope. But they can also be dug into flat ground. The good news is root cellars aren't all that difficult to build. You'll find free building plan links at the end of this chapter. Their average cost for materials is around $1,300, but if you are industrious, you can bargain shop at places like habitat for humanity and discount lumber suppliers. If you're *really* feeling lucky, why not try craigslist for used or free materials?

Although there have been a few experiments that led to moderate success, for the most part root cellars are not effective for conditions where the ground stays warm year round. For such conditions, consider home canning or dehydrating your fruits and vegetables. Food dehydration works well in warm, low humidity climate conditions.

In harsh winter temperatures, where stored foods could freeze, build your root cellar with extra insulation and vents to let in warmer daytime air. Climate zones that experience severe winter temperatures will benefit with a manure pit. Due to its slow decomposition, a manure pit will supply needed heat to keep temperatures in your cellar from dropping below freezing.

Two of the biggest threats to food stored in root cellars are rodents and rot. Rodents can be controlled by installing wire mesh wherever they can enter, especially around air vents. To avoid rot, check food storage regularly, tossing any foods that have begun to spoil. If left unchecked, one spoiled fruit or vegetable can ruin the entire bunch.

## You Should Know

**Root Cellars** don't have to be restricted to just storing fruits and vegetables. Other candidates that benefit from cooler temperatures are nuts, milk, cream, butter, cheese, beans, beer, wine, cured bacon, and other smoked meats. Smoked fish also keeps well in a root cellar.

**Apples** have the longest shelf life of fruits, and for the vegetable, it is the potato. Runners-up for vegetables with a long shelf life are: beans, beets, cabbage, kohlrabi, onions, peppers (dried), pumpkins, nuts, squash (winter), sweet potatoes, and turnips.

**Vegetables** and fruits should be stored unwashed to avoid adding moisture that will promote rot.

**Root Vegetables** such as carrots, beets, and turnips store best in five gallon buckets between layers of slightly damp sand or sawdust.

**Potatoes** have a long storage life, but are best stored in sacks or boxes in the darkest area of your root cellar to avoid their turning green.

**Apples** give off gases that affect other stored goods. They should be kept separately from your other food storage, layered with newspapers in boxes that are relatively tight to keep the gases from escaping.

**Root Crops** should be stored in containers of loose soil or sawdust that protect them from the emissions of other vegetables.

**Cabbages and Onions** give off odors that can be absorbed by vegetables and fruits. They are best stored away from other stored foods.

**Pumpkins and Squash** keep best in cool places at around 55 degrees with 70% to 75% humidity. Storing them in a cool location in your home or stairwell is a solution for long-term storage.

## Individual Fruit and Vegetable Storage Needs

At first glance, it may seem the diverse temperature demands of various fruits and vegetables listed below would not lend themselves to being stored together in a root cellar, but temperatures can rise a full 10 degrees warmer at ceiling height.

Because of this, you will gain optimal variation of temperature and humidity by installing tall shelves in your root cellar. Keep thermometers and hygrometer humidity gauges in several locations on the walls of your cellar to keep an eye on conditions. If you find you need more humidity, sprinkling water on the floor will increase the humidity level. Be sure to watch for high humidity conditions, where condensation may drip from the ceiling and spoil stored food.

## Apples

Cold and moist
Do not store with vegetables
32 to 40 degrees Fahrenheit
80 to 90 percent relative humidity

## Beans

Cool and dry
32 to 50 degrees Fahrenheit
60 to 70 percent relative humidity

## Beets

Cold and very moist
32 to 40 degrees Fahrenheit
90 to 95 percent relative humidity

## Brussels Sprouts

Cold and very moist
32 to 40 degrees Fahrenheit
90 to 95 percent relative humidity

## Cabbage

Cold and very moist
32 to 40 degrees Fahrenheit
90 to 95 percent relative humidity

## Cabbage, Chinese

Cold and very moist
32 to 40 degrees Fahrenheit
90 to 95 percent relative humidity


## Carrots

Cold and very moist
32 to 40 degrees Fahrenheit
90 to 95 percent relative humidity


## Cauliflower

Cold and very moist
32 to 40 degrees Fahrenheit
90 to 95 percent relative humidity


## Celery

Cold and very moist
32 to 40 degrees Fahrenheit
90 to 95 percent relative humidity


## Garlic

Cool and dry
32 to 35 degrees Fahrenheit
60 to 70 percent relative humidity

## Grapefruit

Cold and moist
Do not store with vegetables
32 to 40 degrees Fahrenheit
80 to 90 percent relative humidity

## Grapes

Cold and moist
Do not store with vegetables
32 to 40 degrees Fahrenheit
80 to 90 percent relative humidity

## Jerusalem Artichoke

Cold and very moist
32 to 40 degrees Fahrenheit
90 to 95 percent relative humidity

May be left in the ground undisturbed until needed. Digging can be done unless the soil is frozen hard. A thick layer of mulch may extend your harvest season.

## Kale

Cold and very moist
32 to 40 degrees Fahrenheit
90 to 95 percent relative humidity

## Kohlrabi

Cold and very moist
32 to 40 degrees Fahrenheit
90 to 95 percent relative humidity

## Onions

Cool and dry
32 to 35 degrees Fahrenheit
60 to 70 percent relative humidity

## Oranges

Cold and moist
Do not store with vegetables
32 to 40 degrees Fahrenheit
80 to 90 percent relative humidity

## Parsnips

Cold and very moist
32 to 40 degrees Fahrenheit
90 to 95 percent relative humidity

## Pears

Cold and moist
Do not store with vegetables
32 to 40 degrees Fahrenheit
80 to 90 percent relative humidity

## Peas

Cool and dry
32 to 50 degrees Fahrenheit
60 to 70 percent relative humidity

## Peppers, hot dried

Cool and dry
32 to 50 degrees Fahrenheit
60 to 70 percent relative humidity

## Popcorn

Cool and dry
32 to 50 degrees Fahrenheit
60 to 70 percent relative humidity

## Potatoes

Cold and moist
Do not store with fruits
38 to 40 degrees Fahrenheit ideal
80 to 90 percent relative humidity

## Potatoes, sweet

Warm and moist
50 degrees Fahrenheit
80 to 90 percent relative humidity

## Pumpkins

Warm and dry
50 to 55 degrees Fahrenheit
60 to 75 percent relative humidity

## Radish, winter

Cold and very moist
32 to 40 degrees Fahrenheit
90 to 95 percent relative humidity

## Rutabaga

Cold and very moist
32 to 40 degrees Fahrenheit
90 to 95 percent relative humidity

## Squash, winter

Warm and dry
50 to 55 degrees Fahrenheit
60 to 75 percent relative humidity

## Tomatoes

Warm and moist
50 degrees Fahrenheit
80 to 90 percent relative humidity

**Turnip**

Cold and very moist
32 to 40 degrees Fahrenheit
90 to 95 percent relative humidity

# Home Canning

Home canning is an excellent method for preserving garden foods. When you cannot build a root cellar, it is doubly important to set aside home canning supplies. Winter's realities won't seem nearly as harsh when you have a good stock of fruits and vegetables lining your pantry shelves.

With one or two good canning books, and by following the instructions, it isn't hard to home can. There are really only a few rules, but those rules must be followed in order to avoid bacteria such as Salmonella, Staphylococcus Aurous (staph), and Botulism. These bacteria are sometimes found in low acidic foods: meats, vegetables and beans that can be killed off in a pressure cooker allowed to boil at 240 degrees and held at that temperature for the time specified in your canning recipe. If you live at elevations higher than 1,000 feet above sea level, you will need to adjust the pounds pressure on your pressure cooker according to the chart provided with your recipe.

Fruits are acidic and canning is done by using the boiling water method. A temperature of 212 degrees must be reached for the time indicated in the recipe. As with the steam pressure method, if you live higher than 1,000 feet above sea level, you will need to adjust the processing time according to the chart instructions found in the recipe instructions.

**Rule #1** Never break the rules.

**Rule #2** If your aunt, neighbor, or co-worker shared a great microwave recipe for canning anything, toss it! The same goes for the "aspirin" method, or anything else that doesn't include either a pressure cooker for non-acidic foods, or a boiling water canner method for acidic foods. Using any other method means you may be playing games with your health.

**Rule #3** If the same aunt, neighbor, or co-worker who shared the microwave recipe gives you some great antique glass lids with jar rubbers, make them into attractive spice jars for your bulk spices, but don't use them for canning. Antique glass lids with jar rubbers make it impossible to double check that a tight seal has been obtained, therefore there will be no way to know if your food is safe to eat. Likewise, do not use pickle jars, mayonnaise jars, or any jars that were not specifically designed for canning use. They will not give your canning the safe seal you need and any food canned in them will need to be thrown out.

**Rule #4** Never re-use metal lids. They are designed for one use, and trying to sneak past this rule will yield canned food that spoils and will make you sick. If you will be canning during a protracted crisis, get plenty of lids.

Possibly the most difficult part of canning at a time when the stores may not be open is taking an educated guess at the amount of jars and lids to put aside. Because canning will be a lifeline during troubled times, I would suggest putting aside more than you feel you will need. And then, add more for the sake of Murphy's Law. There is a great supplier of plastic re-usable canning lids called Tattler Reusable Lids. The prices are higher than traditional lids, but because they can be reused for years, they take the guesswork out of planning ahead for home canning. Their link is provided at the end of this chapter.

Luckily, jars are reusable as long as their rims are not chipped, where the sealing process during canning would be compromised.

Below is a list of canning supplies you will need. Many of the items shown, you may already have on hand. Items like a large crock pot to ferment pickles and sauerkraut may not be necessary if you don't happen to like either. Glass canning jars come in several sizes: wide-mouth jars, regular-mouth jars and jelly jars. Once you have the chance to sit down with your canning recipe book, look it over and brainstorm what you're likely to be canning.

## Canning Supply List

Boiling-Water Canner
Canning Jars
Canning Funnel
Caps, Two Piece
Cheesecloth, Food Grade
Chef's Knife
Colander
Cooking Timer
Cooks Spoon
Corer
Crock
Cutting Boards
Food Mill, Manual
Food Scale
Grater
Jar Lifter
Jelly Bag & Stand
Kitchen Towels
Ladle

Large Saucepot
Lid Wand
Measuring Cups
Measuring Spoons
Paring Knife
Plastic Spatula
Pot Holders
Potato Masher
Pressure-Cooker Canner
Rubber Spatulas
Saucepan
Skimmer
Spice Bag
Tongs
Wire Basket
Wooden Spoons
Vegetable Peeler
Zester

## Dehydrating Foods

Food dehydration has been in use since the beginning of man when meat was dried in caves for survival. Electric food dehydrators can be counted on as long as the electrical grid is up. If you plan to have a garden and do not have a root cellar, or canning supplies, food dehydration will be your saving grace.

Investing in a book on dehydration will give you the confidence to preserve your food. For the time being, know that your food must be as dry as possible for dehydrated foods to store well, or it will grow mold and will have to be thrown out. Dehydrated food can be stored in glass jars with screw down lids or in zip-lock bags. Watch for any condensation collecting in containers. If you see visible signs of condensation, the food will have to be re-dehydrated right away, before it has the chance to grow mold.

There is another solution for food dehydration that will require a little do-it-yourself. You can build one by following the DYI instructions link provided at the end of this chapter.

# List of Suggested Suppliers and Reading Material

**Note:** Although the author has studied, and in some cases ordered from the following suggested sites, it is always wise to do your own research for the best pricing and availability for your geographic location. At the time of the publication of *Survival: Prepare Before Disaster Strikes,* each site listed was operational.

## Eco Fan Supplier

http://www.garrettwade.com/product.asp?pn=25T05.01&SID=W6061 003&EID=Garrett%20Wade&gclid=CJDArt6v3akCFQY-bAodZCvWZg

## Do-It-Yourself Food Dehydrator

http://ecobites.com/diy-recycling-projects/712?task=view

http://www.rootsimple.com/2008/10/build-solar-dehydrator.html

## Do-It-Yourself Root Cellar

*Instructions to Build a Root Cellar From Wooden Pallets*
http://theepicenter.com/tow1102.html

http://www.survival-spot.com/survival-blog/build-root-cellar/

*Earth Bag Constructed for Around $300*
http://www.motherearthnews.com/Do-It-Yourself/Earthbag-Building-Garden-Shed.aspx

*Inexpensively Made With Barrels or Trashcans*
http://www.saveourskills.com/?s=root+cellar+ideas

*Build a Basement Root Cellar*
http://www.motherearthnews.com/do-it-yourself/basement-root-cellar-zm0z04zsie.aspx

http://www.organicgardening.com/learn-and-grow/building-root-cellar

## Links to Home Canning Advice, Supplies & Recipes

*Huge Selection of Canning Recipes*
http://www.pickyourown.org/allaboutcanning.htm

http://www.freshpreserving.com/

http://www.canningpantry.com/home-canning-recipes.html

## Tattler Reusable Canning Lids

http://www.amazon.com/Tattler-Reusable-Regular-Canning-Rubber/dp/B0051PDXCQ

## Links to Do-It-Yourself Food Dehydrators

http://ecobites.com/diy-recycling-projects/712?task=view

http://www.rootsimple.com/2008/10/build-solar-dehydrator.html

## Links to Information on Food Dehydration Methods

*Detailed Information on Food Dehydration*
http://farmgal.tripod.com/Dehydrate.html

http://www.all-things-emergency-prepared.com/how-to-dehydrate-food.html

# Chapter 15

# Lighting & Waste Disposal

*"The human body is the only machine for which
there are no spare parts."*
Hermann Biggs

Each subject within this chapter could be thought of as the catchall drawer we all have. We may not want to think about them, but we couldn't live without them. Where else would we throw that key that goes *somewhere,* and that one extra battery that came with the 4-pack, or the loose change and the little thing-a-ma-gig that looks important, but who knows?

So it is with lighting, laundry, bathing, garbage disposal, and toilet facilities. Right now, things are under control; we flip a switch and there's light; we need to use the facilities and we don't think anything of a flushing toilet; we throw our garbage into the garbage bin, and provided we've paid the garbage bill, it's picked up weekly.

But when you think about it, all of these creature comforts are contingent on the power that runs to our homes and on gasoline supplies being readily available and on our water supply—either well water that's contingent upon electricity to run the water pump or the water municipality—to deliver water to our faucets, toilets, and bathtubs *and* we also assume that our sinks and tubs will drain.

Should any of these infrastructures fail, it's going to be a very bad day for anyone who hasn't planned ahead.

## Toilet Facilities

If you live in an urban setting, it's highly unlikely you will have access to an outhouse. In the suburbs and rural settings, an outhouse becomes a distinct possibility. Many areas have strict rules against an outhouse due to CCR's and city health code regulations. If this is an issue for your area, then you may want to purchase the materials for one and build it when services have ceased and it's much less likely building inspectors will be running around, checking for non-compliance—they might be just as busy as you building their own outhouses!

In Chapter 2, *Are You Ready?*, this issue was addressed. Here in Chapter 15, think of it as a "gentle reminder". When I first mentioned building an outhouse to my brother, he did a fairly good job of dancing around the issue, mumbling something about nailing a couple of tarps between a few trees deep in the woods and calling it good. Poor guy. When his wife and I were through giving the many reasons why this wouldn't work: bear, coyote, wolf, moose, sub-freezing weather, lack of privacy, and several small children in the group, he threw up his hands in defeat.

The moral here is that whether it's convenient or not, you should make plans for bathroom facilities. Visit the links for DIY plans on building an outhouse at the end of this chapter and set aside the materials you will need. At some point, if infrastructure breaks down and all you have is an outhouse, you'll be the bell of the ball in your neighborhood! If you live in an urban setting, you will want to dig a hole outdoors for waste. Just make sure to buy a camp toilet, a folding shovel, and plenty of plastic bags.

## Keep It Clean

You will want to arrange for bathing and sponge baths. Don't expect to be able to use a bathtub or sink unless you have a septic system and a manual hand pump to provide plentiful water. If you depend upon municipal water, your tubs and sinks will not drain once the power supply runs out. It is possible to set up bathtubs and sinks for "gray water", meaning water that is diverted from the tub and sink to the outdoors or to outdoor holding tanks that can be made out of 55-gallon food-grade barrels (refer to Chapter 3, under the heading *Water Containment Systems*). It is possible to re-use gray water for gardening use by using soaps and shampoos that do not contain sodium, chlorine or boron, as these chemicals will harm plants. Instead, store low-phosphate, biodegradable soaps and detergents. Unless you are handy at plumbing, converting to a gay water system will need to be done by a plumber. Tread cautiously. There may be restrictions against gray water systems in the city and some rural locations.

If setting up for gray water would be prohibitive, tough stuff tubs aren't expensive and will allow for the water to be carried out and used for gardening needs after bathing, dish duty, or laundry. Because portable washtubs have long gone out of fashion, a horse trough or feeder that is watertight will also suffice. They can be found at feed or farm supply stores. Purchase them locally to avoid shipping costs. Portable solar camp showers are also a good alternative for use during warm weather conditions.

At the end of this chapter you will find the link to free DIY instructions to build a simple, inexpensive washing machine. You will also find links to manual washing machines and a manual spin clothes dryer. Be sure to put aside plenty of body soap, shampoo, dish soap and laundry soap to see you through. And don't forget to add clothesline and clothes pegs to your preparedness goods list!

Bathing probably won't be daily—not when precious water must be saved for drinking and cooking—so get plenty of wet wash-ups for quick cleaning between baths.

## Lighting

It was not uncommon for frontier families to go to bed when it turned dark and wake up to the crow of a rooster. It was a sensible plan, as Mother Nature provided lighting and they had farm animals that had to be tended to and other chores to do in the early morning hours.

In today's world, even when confronted with the changes brought on by a crisis, we may not be able to turn off our internal clocks to accommodate for a lack of natural light. The good news is the solution is sitting on the shelf of a preparedness supplier or camping supply outlet.

**Candles** are obvious choices, particularly long-burning, emergency candles. Safety can be an issue when there are small children to be considered. Luckily, glass hurricane candle holders are an easy fix and some styles are wall mountable.

**Oil lamps** are another inexpensive, efficient solution for lighting. They burn either paraffin oil or kerosene; however, kerosene should be stored in a shed or a detached garage, away from an open flame source. Aladdin lamps burn six times as bright as do most other lamps and do not smoke or throw off odors because they burn with air pressure. The downside to Aladdin lamps is they consume twice as much kerosene or paraffin oil.

Oil lamps are available in wall-mount and table surface models. How much paraffin oil or kerosene you will need to store depends upon the model and your specific lighting needs. Be sure to purchase plenty of replacement wicks and replacement chimneys.

**Battery-run lanterns** are another alternative to electric lighting. If you live in a climate zone that has plenty of sunshine, a solar powered battery charger will circumvent the need to put aside a large cache of batteries.

**Solar powered** is another possibility, especially for those who live in sunny climates. If you expect to be doing close work like sewing or reading, be aware that solar lighting may not offer sufficient lighting for these tasks, so plan to add at least a couple of oil lamps.

**Outdoor camp lanterns** are meant solely for the outdoors. They give off carbon monoxide and are not safe for indoor use, although they are great for outdoor tasks.

**Flashlights** In a prolonged crisis, where the grocery and hardware stores may be closed, you will need a couple of battery-run flashlights and a cache of batteries (look into solar battery chargers), and several non-battery, shakable flashlights. Headlamps are great conveniences that leave your hands free for tasks. They are almost essential when you find yourself needing to do fix-ups or tend to animals once the sun has gone down.

# List of Suggested Suppliers and Reading Material

**Note:** Although the author has studied, and in some cases ordered from the following suggested sites, it is always wise to do your own research for the best pricing and availability for your geographic location. At the time of the publication of *Survival: Prepare Before Disaster Strikes,* each site listed was operational.


## Lighting

*36 and 120-Hour Emergency Candles*
http://www.nitro-pak.com/catalogsearch/result/?q=candle&x=0&y=0

*5-Hour Candles and Flashlights*
http://www.quakekare.com/

*Candles, Candle Lanterns, Oil Lanterns*
http://preparedness.com/cancanlam.html

*Candles, Regular Flashlights, Shakable Flashlights*
http://www.iprepare.com/candlesmatches.html

*Oil lanterns—all styles*
http://www.Lehmans.com

*Hurricane Oil Lamps*
http://www.ask.com/web?qsrc=1&o=0&l=dir&q=hurricane+oil+lamps

*Oil Lanterns and Kerosene Blackout Lamps*
http://www.lanternnet.com/


## Bathing Needs

*Six-Gallon Feeder (suitable for alternative bathing)*
http://www.horse.com/item/fortiflex-feed-tub/BSA25/

*Tuff Stuff Oval Bathing Buckets*
http://www.4fishstuff.com/index.php?cPath=54_221

## Laundry Needs

*Lehman's Sells This Laundry Plunger and Other Manual Laundry Tubs and Wringers*
http://www.lehmans.com/store/Home_Goods___Laundry___Washing ___Rapid_Laundry_Washer___66RW#66RW

*Do-It-Yourself Washing Machine Made from a Bucket and Plunger*
http://www.off-grid.net/2010/04/22/diy-washing-machine-and-homemade-laundry-soap/

*Manual Non-electric Washing Machine*
http://www.laundry-alternative.com/products/Wonderwash.html

*Another Source for a Manual, Off-grid Washing Machine and Manual Spin-dry Clothes Dryer*
http://www.laundry-alternative.com/

## DIY Outhouse

http://www.small-cabin.com/small-cabin-build-other-structures.html

# Chapter 16

# Keeping Farm Animals

*"I have been studying the traits and dispositions of the 'lower animals'
and contrasting them with the traits and dispositions of man.
I find the result humiliating to me."*
Mark Twain

In this chapter, you'll find basic information on raising chickens, goats, cows, pigs, horses, and sheep, including their housing and feeding requirements. It is designed as a way for you to investigate what farm animals might fit with your lifestyle and property.

## Free-Range Chickens

Free-range chickens lend themselves more to self-sufficiency than do caged chickens, so let's start there.

You will need an acre or two of land to provide forging for a flock of free-rangers. If you expect to be living in an urban area, you will want to skip this section altogether and read the following section on caged chickens. In some cases, rural conditions will not provide the bugs, seed and wild grasses necessary for free-range chickens to thrive. Look around. Do those living close by keep free-rangers? Are there turkeys or quail foraging in your area? If so, it's safe to assume your chickens will thrive, but you will want to watch the situation closely at first.

There are reasons other than financial to choose free-rangers. Their eggs contain 1/3 less cholesterol, 1/4 less fat, 2/3 more vitamin A, 2 times more omega-3 fatty acids, three times more vitamin E, and 7 times more beta-carotene. Free-range chickens can forage for around half of their supper until winter months, particularly true in northern climates when foraging beneath snow is impossible. Whether you decide on free-range or caged chickens, you'll need to buy…you guessed it, a couple of books on raising them. One on their care and feeding, specific to either free-range or caged chickens, and the other a veterinary manual, such as the Merck Veterinary Manual. It has an in-depth section on chicken diseases and gives detailed information on how to care for injured birds. Doctoring your flock will save you vet bills now, and prepare you for the future, when it may not be possible to reach a vet. Be sure to put aside the medicines recommended for disease control for your flock.

As with every decision we make regarding self-sufficiency, thinking smart means preparing for a future that may not offer the conveniences we enjoy now. You will need to decide if growing your own feed has the return you will benefit from later on. Plan for it to take between 1 to 1 1/2 acres of corn, depending upon the size of your flock. Many of us will not have the land to devote to growing corn. The good news is chicken feed is around $10 for 100 lbs. When possible, you should put aside one year's worth of feed, so if there comes a time when feed is unobtainable, you can continue to supplement your flock as they adjust to working overtime for their meals.

If your flock is big enough, you may decide to sell extra eggs, which can cover your expenses while still providing plentiful eggs for your own table. If you'd rather put the overflow aside for the winter months when egg production is greatly diminished, refer to *How to Preserve Eggs* found in Chapter 17, *What's for Dinner?*

It's best to get day-old chicks from a hatchery that has been recommended to you. Ask neighbors who keep chickens; they'll be able to provide sound advice that may save you the frustration of choosing the wrong source or breed of chicks. It's advisable to choose a scrappy breed that hasn't had the instinct for survival of living off the land bred out of them. They should also be a breed that thrives in your climate zone. If you plan on using your flock for meat as well as eggs, then you'll want to investigate a meat breed.

Animal predation cannot be completely avoided and the loss of a flock's only rooster would mean replenishing your flock with chicks might not be possible. For this reason, it is wise to subscribe to an heir and a spare, so that if a rooster ends up being a coyote's dinner, your flock will continue to thrive. Because roosters can be aggressive, many homesteaders shy away from keeping more than one, but when planning for survival it's worth considering the added challenge in exchange for a thriving flock.

Chicks are best raised by keeping them in heated stock tanks, or when on a tight budget, raising them in a draft-free location in your home. Timing is important. If you get your chicks in summer, they will have time to grow large enough to roost, producing smaller eggs at first, but larger ones by the next spring. As the chicks get older, and no longer require a heat source, they can be moved to small outdoor cages. Although some keep free-range chickens out in the open, it's safest to provide a wire enclosure for times when they aren't foraging. This better protects them from predators. Those that keep their free-rangers more exposed typically depend upon a watchdog to drive off predators. Such a dog needs to be trained or they, too, may develop a craving for chicken.

The chicken coop can be kept simple, but must have brooding boxes. Typically 4 hens will share a 2-foot X 2-foot brooding box. Make certain you have provided enough brooding space for the number of hens you plan to keep, or they may begin to lay out in the field, which will draw predators to your property. The brooding boxes should be mounted off the floor, allowing room beneath them for chickens to move about. Build a ramp running from the ground to the boxes so your hens can reach them with ease. Brooding boxes should be installed in a dark location away from drafts.

They should be enclosed on three sides with the front left open for hens to get in and out with ease. The coop and brooding area must have a sound roof, so your flock can stay out of the rain. You will need to provide plentiful water in freeze-proof containers (think solar) and a feeder that is protected from vermin.

The ground of the enclosure itself will need to provide at least one square foot, preferably two, of space per chicken to roam.

Although the mother hen is the best way to hatch eggs without electricity, if there will be a large numbers of eggs, kerosene-powered incubators are available at Lehman's for around $400—the link has been provided at the end of this chapter.

For the first month, chicks are fed chick feed, which is slightly medicated to stave off disease. As they get a little older, it's time to begin training them to go out in the field in the daytime, and return to the coop at night. Once the birds are fully grown, feed them once a day at dusk for 1 to 1 ½ hours and then take away the feed. This will encourage them to forage for their own food of bugs, seeds and grasses. As mentioned, there must always be a source of fresh water kept in a freeze-proof container.

You will want to water your flock out in the field if you don't have a natural water source. Otherwise, they may decide to spend the day lazing around the coop, expecting you to supply their feed.

Training your flock takes patience and time, but once you're successful, plan on spending around 1 hour a week on maintenance.

Expect around a 10% natural attrition of your flock. When you see anything worrisome with one of your chickens, like bloody stool or lethargy, it's time to refer to a veterinary manual such as the Merck Veterinary Manual.

**Note**: Free-range chickens can be as heartless as deer with regards to a garden! To avoid their decimating your crop, hang poultry netting, hung loosely between stakes surrounding the garden.


## Caged Chickens

Caged chickens require more food and plenty of room to roam, as they will not have the benefit of exploring out in the field. Caged chickens aren't as exposed to the dangers of predators as long as care is taken when building their coop. Caged chickens should be given 2 square feet of coop space per chicken. This will prevent egg eating and cannibalism. As with free-range chickens, brooding boxes are best built up off the floor around 2 feet from the ground with sufficient room for hens to lay their eggs. The coop must have good insulation to avoid the buildup of toxic fumes and should be well insulated against the elements. Flooring must be kept clean and is best made of concrete to help keep vermin away that will eat your flock's feed and may carry disease. Give your chickens somewhere to roost, as chickens prefer to sleep off the ground. Make sure there are sufficient feeders and waterers to provide for your flock. Adding a chicken run will lead to happy chickens but be sure the wire enclosure is sturdy enough to keep predators out.

## Goats

Cave drawings depicted goats over 2,000 years ago. They were the first domesticated animal besides sheep and dogs and are every bit as important today as they were then. There are a mind boggling 600 breeds of goat, but for the purpose of self-sufficiency in the U.S., we need only discuss a few breeds.

Goat farming can be broken down to three purposes: dairy production (milk, cheese, and yogurt), meat and wool. Common breeds found in the United States are Toggenburg, French Alpine, Saanen, Nubian, and the LaMancha breed that are used for dairy. Boers, their larger cousin, are raised for meat. Other meat goat breeds are Kiko, Savanna, and Mytonic. Angoras are bred for their wool.

Goats are one of the more affordable farm animals to raise, as their milk can be produced for pennies on the gallon. Does can produce 1 to 3 kids a year. During a protracted crisis, there are worse things than being the owner of goats. But if you choose goats, buy a friend. They are social creatures and they need companionship.

As with free-range chickens, goats will forage for their own food, but must be supplemented with hay and oats. They will produce milk, cheese, yogurt, butter (although a bit hard to make) and meat, and their waste provides rich fertilizer for the garden. Goats can be counted on to yield nearly one gallon of milk a day and their eating requirements are just a fraction of a cow's—and the reason why goats are called the poor man's cow. If your family cannot consume a gallon of milk every day, the excess can go to feed other farm animals. Chickens and pigs love goat's milk.

It makes economic sense to select the breed of goat most common to your area, as they will sell easier when it comes time to part with extra kids.

A goat's minimalist eating requirements flows over to their enclosure needs as well. A shed with three sides that keeps the weather out that faces south is acceptable. Generally, providing 16 square feet for each animal will give goats enough room to be content. Goats love to jump, so plan on building a sturdy fence, able to withstand their hoofs, and built at least 5-foot high to foil the best of escape artists. However, it's worth building a taller fence if your area gets heavy snowfall, where drifts might offer an escape route for goats. You'll find links for free online building plans for goat enclosures at the end of this chapter.

Plan on feeding your goats hay with a bit of grain, and let them forage for at least some of their food. During breeding season, bucks benefit from 1 to 2 pounds of grain a day, and pregnant does should be given 1 to 2 pounds of grain a day—the amount increasing as she nears the end of her pregnancy.

There aren't many health-related requirements for goats, but hoof trimming must be done monthly. To ignore this can cause them to go lame. De-budding should be done when goats are young, as their horns are mere buds at that point and easier to remove. Castration of the males you don't intend to breed is another aspect of maintaining a goat herd.

As for selecting your goat, do your research. A good approach is to attend shows where you can familiarize yourself with what to look for.

A book on goats is another source to familiarize yourself with the different breeds and their uses. If you're lucky enough to have neighbors who raise goats, it wouldn't hurt to ask their advice on breed selection.

# Cows

There is no doubt about it, cows are the Mercedes of milk production and can be counted to provide 5 to 10 gallons of milk a day. Their milk will also provide butter, ice cream, cheese, yogurt, and cottage cheese. The compost pile and garden loves their by-products, too. But beware: cows need between 25 to 50 gallons of water a day. This is where having a natural water source or a well is mandatory.

During the growing months, providing 1 to 2 acres of rich grassland is enough to provide for their keep. In winter, or when you cannot provide rich grassland, you will need to feed a mature cow approximately 1/3 to 1/2 bale of hay each day, along with a little grain. Hay prices vary depending upon location. For most homesteaders, having the acreage available to produce that much hay is prohibitive. If you live near a farmer you may be able to barter for hay, but for that to work you'll have to have something worth their while.

Feeding cows apples or table scraps can cause bloat, evidenced with a ridged stomach and foaming at the mouth. A cow's digestive system is not designed to handle processing such roughage, and bloat means calling the vet or it can lead to death.

When choosing a dairy cow, you will want to be certain she is not only healthy, but gentle as well. There isn't a more unpleasant experience than getting kicked in the chest when trying to milk Bessie! Only research and familiarizing yourself on what breeds do best in your climate zone will give you the information you need to choose the right breed of cow. Attend cattle auctions and listen and learn from the experts. If you can, take along someone who has experience with cows. You'll be tending and milking your cow for 10 to 15 years so it is important to get a healthy milker; one that will not be a drain on your finances with vet bills—assuming you can locate a vet during times of unrest. It's good practice to test run a cow before shelling out the cash by milking her first.

Cows don't necessarily have to have a fancy barn, unless you happen to live in Alaska where winter temperatures can be counted to dip well below the sub-zero range. When providing an open-ended cattle shed, their enclosures must allow them to get out of the rain and snow, and in summer, the hot sun. You should plan for around 60 square feet of space for each adult cow, and 30 to 40 square feet for calves. The shed should face south for the cow to benefit from sunlight in the winter months. Bedding is something that needs to be planned for, as cow bedding amounts to approximately one ton of hay per cow annually. Forty inches of sturdy fencing will suffice to keep a cow contained.

The most popular breeds of dairy cows are Ayrshire, Brown Swiss, Guernsey, Holstein, and Jersey. Dual-purpose cows that provide both milk and meat are Devon, Dexter, Dutch Belted, and Shorthorn. If you're uncomfortable with the idea of keeping such a large animal (they weigh between 1,000 to 1,200 lbs), you might consider a smaller breed such as the Dexter.

Another breed extremely popular with homesteaders are the mini-Jersey. They are much smaller than a full-sized cow, ranging from 38" to 42" at the shoulder when full grown, and weigh between 600 to 700 lbs. Their drawback is they are hard to find because of their demand and they fetch higher prices than do most cows. These miniatures need a mineral lick available to them at all times. They require less feed and have gentle dispositions. But don't let their smaller size fool you. They are great milk producers, usually producing 4 gallons of milk a day or more.

## Horses

Horses are a favorite for many of us. Hopefully a horse would never be seen as a source of meat, but they will provide transportation. During a time of prolonged crisis, having a quiet, efficient mode of transportation would be very useful.

It goes without saying that the amount a horse eats depends upon its size and how active it is. Generally, a one thousand pound horse will eat approximately 20 to 30 lbs of food a day, with 3/4 of their food coming from hay or pasture grass. A working draft horse will require more feed than a less active horse that may get by on 15 lbs of grass or hay each day. The remainder of their food requirements includes oats, bran, sweet feed, and grain—but not too much grain, or they'll get sick. They require 10 to 12 gallons of water on cool days and between 20 to 25 gallons of water in hot weather.

During the winter months, particularly in northern climates, grazing on pastureland may not be possible and their food source will be almost exclusively hay; and the reason why keeping a horse is a big financial and logistic commitment, especially for a small-hold homesteader.

Unless you believe you could handle bareback riding, a horse requires a saddle, a saddle blanket, reins, a bit, and a halter.

Horses are fairly high maintenance, as they require a furriers visit every three months to check the condition of their hooves. They should be groomed daily, which includes picking their hooves of debris. They are not loaners and should have companionship. It's not unusual to find a small-hold farmer letting his goats, or sheep, or even a cow keep them company. Horses must be allowed a pasture. To confine them to an enclosure day after day is cruel to a horse and may lead to physiological issues.

Horses can experience colic, which if left untreated, may lead to death. Other heath concerns are lameness, hoof wall loss, hoof crack, and dental issues. When purchasing a horse, it is important to bring along an experienced horseman or a veterinarian. Unless you are an experienced rider, it's a good idea to shy away from a stallion. Look into mares and gildings, as they tend to be less spirited and are easier to ride. Undesirable traits are nipping, biting, and unwillingness to follow your lead when riding. Many times these traits are difficult if not impossible to break.

**Note:** There are many breeds of horses and their costs fluctuate depending upon the breed. During the current economic challenges, owners are sometimes forced to sell their horse at a greatly reduced price, and can be found for free in certain cases.

# Pigs

Pigs are a great source of protein. From piglets, it typically takes 5 months before they reach the weight of 200 lbs and are ready for slaughter, providing you with ham, bacon, pork roast, picnic shoulder, pork chops, sausage, salt pork, and lard. They also provide excellent fertilizer for the garden. It isn't suggested to raise a pig past 200 lbs, as the weight they put on from there is more likely to be fat than meat.

Shade is very important to a pig, as they can't sweat, nor can they pant well to cool themselves. A three-sided enclosure will suffice to house pigs, built with 20 square feet of shade per pig. Fencing is tricky because pigs have great snouts to search out a weak link to escape. It takes extremely sturdy wire fencing, and possibly a trench filled with rocks, to barricade and stop pigs from tunneling to freedom.

Attending livestock shows and county fairs, or getting to know a neighbor who raises pigs will help educate you on what to look for in a piglet before buying one. It isn't advisable to pick a runt for its "better" price. Timing is everything with regards to raising piglets, and it's best done while your garden is yielding, so leftovers and extra table scraps can go to the pig. Early winter is the optimal time for slaughtering and butchering.

Pigs are not finicky eaters and will gladly consume eggs (spoiled or not), fruit, garden clippings, meat scraps, milk, weeds, and vegetables. That's the good news. The bad news is a growing pig can eat up to 60 lbs of slop a day. This typically means you will need to provide grain or commercial pig food that contains at least 20% protein. A pig does best with vitamin and mineral supplements. As with all livestock pigs require plentiful water, around 3 gallons a day.

Pigs are prone to internal parasites and should be wormed every 4 to 6 weeks. External parasites must be dealt with using an insecticide that is available in organic form if preferred.


# Sheep

Sheep come with interesting trivia. They were used for milk production before the cow. There are many breeds of sheep, with some breeds being better for meat production, and others for dairy. Sheep yield less milk than do cows or goats, but with regards to the East Friesian breed, the best producers of the dairy sheep, they will provide from 160 gallons to close to 400 gallons per lactation period. Other breeds will produce from 100 gallons to 200 gallons of milk per lactation period. If you're looking for a dairy sheep, prices for East Friesian's start at around $400 a head.

Sheep milk is richer in vitamins A, B, and E, calcium, phosphorus, potassium, and magnesium than cow's milk. Because the fat globules in sheep milk are smaller than what is found in cow's milk, sheep milk is easier to digest. Their milk is traditionally made into cheese such as Feta, Ricotta, Romano, and Roquefort (depending upon the country making it), as it contains around 7% fat, opposed to cows milk, which is approximately 3.35% fat, and is higher in protein and calcium. Their rich milk is also used to make yogurt and ice cream.

Like goats, sheep are nature's lawn mowers. They are grazers, and tend to munch down to the root of grass, clover and weeds. If you live in a wet climate zone, where vegetation grows profusely, then you can plan on keeping up to 10 sheep on just one acre of land. For arid conditions, reverse this to one sheep for ten acres. Providing an enclosure is a must. Grown sheep aren't generally bothered by rain, but they need shade in hot weather. Lambs, however, do not do well in cold, wet weather conditions. Fencing must keep predators out, as sheep are vulnerable to predators, and are not known to have the tools to defend themselves. This issue requires double fencing. The outside fence is made of barbed wire, strung low to the ground and tall enough to avoid predation. The interior fence requirement is not as stringent, as they are used to separate animals such as ewes from lambs, and rams from ewes. With both exterior and interior fencing, electric fencing is typically installed, but when preparing for life off the electrical grid, this may not be possible. You can always start with electrical fencing, to teach your sheep to respect fencing, and later, such measures will not be as necessary, as they will have learned to respect their enclosure's parameters. Solar fencing is another solution for fencing needs.

For northern climates, you will need to feed a 100 lb ewe around 4 lbs of hay each day when wintertime does not provide their normal pasture grazing. For a treat, they love grain, but beware: they'll eat until they get sick, so watch how much you give them. Their watering requirements are approximately one gallon a day, and this will increase in particularly hot weather.

Sheep must be sheared annually, or twice annually, depending upon the breed and the climactic conditions, unless they are a hair breed like a Barbados. Sheep must have their tails docked for hygienic reasons. Anyone shearing sheep must learn how to do it correctly to avoid cuts and abrasions, or otherwise stressing the animal. As with all farm animals, sheep require vaccinations and they need to be wormed at least twice a year. Pregnant ewes and their lambs are given three vaccinations: BoSe, which is a vitamin-mineral supplement, as well as tetanus and enterotoxaemia (to safeguard against overheating disease). A sheep's hooves must be trimmed and periodically checked for foot rot—a fungus caused by standing in wet conditions. A good book that includes health maintenance for your sheep is advisable, so that if a vet is unavailable, you'll be able to care for them yourself.

# List of Suggested Suppliers and Reading Material

**Note:** Although the author has studied, and in some cases ordered from the following suggested sites, it is always wise to do your own research for the best pricing and availability for your geographic location. At the time of the publication of *Survival: Prepare Before Disaster Strikes,* each site listed was operational.

## Suggested Websites & Reading

*Merck Veterinary Manual—Great all-inclusive manual on animal husbandry*
http://www.merckvetmanual.com/mvm/index.jsp

*Informative Magazine Related to Raising Chickens*
http://www.practicalpoultry.com

*Website about Organic Farming*
http://www.countryfarm-lifestyles.com/index.html

*Site Devoted to Keeping Goats*
http://www.keeping-goats.com/

*Blog all about Chickens*
http://www.avianaquamiser.com/news/

*Information on Raising Chickens*
http://www.backyardchickens.com/

## Non-Electric Farm Equipment

*Non-electric Preparedness Goods, including farm implements and books*
http://www.lehmans.com

## Do-It-Yourself Goat Enclosure

http://makingdowiththenotsonew.blogspot.com/2008/11/goat-shelter-from-lumber-scraps.html


## Chicken Coops

*Large Selection of DIY Chicken Coop Pictorials and Retail Chicken Coops*
http://www.backyardchickens.com/coopdesigns.html

*Free Chicken Coop Plans*
http://howtobuildachickencoopplans.com/

# Chapter 17

# What's for Dinner?

*"I've been on a constant diet for the last two decades.*
*I've lost a total of 789 pounds.*
*By all accounts, I should be hanging from a charm bracelet. "*
Erma Bombeck

A good supply of food storage related recipes are a must-have. There are excellent cookbooks written specifically for cooking with bulk foods and I recommend you purchase a few. If you are on a tight budget, look online for used food storage cookbooks or surf the web for survival, preparedness, and camping websites and blogs—some of which have been added at the end of this chapter. They often share recipes for cooking with bulk foods. Some survival food suppliers provide recipes for use with bulk storage food as well. If you haven't already started a recipe collection, now is a good time to start. Just be sure to download them because in a grid-down situation with your computer on lock-down, you'll be sunk.

If you haven't found the time to practice cooking with your food storage, begin now. It takes time and experience to come up with meals that are tasty if you aren't already practiced at cooking with home storage. Cooking with home storage once or twice a week will introduce the change of diet to your family slowly, so when having to revert solely to home storage when disaster strikes, the transition will not be as harsh—especially for young children and the elderly.

Information for non-refrigerated methods for preserving sourdough starter, eggs, and cheese are included in this chapter.

It's a good idea to begin your sourdough starter now to familiarize yourself with its care and feeding. For the procrastinators out there who never quite got around to buying yeast or getting a sourdough starter going (I know you're out there), I've included recipes for Irish soda, spoon, and quick bread that do not require yeast.

At the end of this chapter are a few inexpensive ideas to keep your child occupied, including a recipe for finger paints and Play Dough. Be sure to have zip-lock bags or plastic containers with lids on hand to store it.

## Preserving Eggs

Believe it or not, eggs do not require refrigeration when stored properly. Now, before you throw down this book, convinced if you follow the instructions on preserving eggs, you are doomed, consider the plight of our ancestors. They had to find a way to press through the long winter months when their hens stopped or slowed down on their egg laying—dependent on how cooperative they were and whether they suffered from seasonal disorder disease (okay, now I'm being cheeky).

The following water glass method for storing eggs for 6 to 9 months—plenty of time to make it to the other side of winter—is, in my opinion one of the best methods our ancestors used to preserve eggs.

## Directions

Follow directions carefully and use crocks or glass containers such as one-half or gallon-sized containers with screw cap lids. The top should be hermetically sealed with paraffin or Vaseline-coated paper. Do not use glass-topped containers, as silicate can cement the lid closed, making them impossible to open.

You will be using one-part water glass per ten-parts boiled water. Water glass can be purchased at Lehman's listed in the links at the end of this chapter. I have heard pharmacy's can order it, but I didn't test that theory, so if it turns out to be a myth, please don't kill the messenger! Half-gallon containers will usually hold up to 15 eggs, and gallon-sized containers will hold approximately 30 eggs. It will be necessary to do the math for your boiled water needs, as this is determined based on how many containers you intend to put up.

Use only fresh eggs and if possible, preserve them the same day they are laid. This is suggested because you will be using farm-fresh eggs and a fertilized egg begins incubation when they are kept for about twenty-four hours in temperatures of at least 80 degrees. Following a 24-hour rule, you need not worry about spoilage.

**DO NOT** use washed eggs (this immediately excludes grocery store eggs as they are commercially washed). Farm-fresh eggs still retain their "bloom", the coating placed on them by the hen while being laid that protects them from outside pollutants. Gently wipe off any unwanted residue with a dry, soft cloth. Never use water, and, I repeat, never wash them.

Carefully inspect eggs for cracks or chips, and if found, do not use it, for it *will* spoil, ruining the whole bunch!

Let the water cool and then place the eggs into the 1:10 ratio of water glass point side down.

As soon as the eggs are packed in the preserving liquid with between 1-2 inches of liquid covering the top eggs, the receptacle should be carefully sealed with a paraffin or Vaseline treated paper or pasteboard, or with a screw cap or another reliable, tight cover. This is necessary not only to prevent water from volatilizing, which would expose the top-most eggs to the atmosphere and spoiling the whole bunch, but also to prevent the carbonic acid of the air from decomposing the silicate in the water glass protecting them.

Store in a cool, dark place.

## Preserving Eggs with Shortening or Vaseline

You can use either Vaseline or a Crisco-type shortening (that does not contain animal fat) to preserve eggs. Start with farm-fresh eggs that have not had the "bloom" washed from them—which excludes the eggs you find at the grocery store that have been commercially washed. Gently wipe away any residue with a soft dry cloth. Next coat them with either Vaseline, or Crisco, wiping off any excess. This closes the eggshell to the air and prevents the egg from spoiling. Eggs can be stored with this method for approximately 1 month.

Eggs preserved with the Vaseline/shortening method must be turned daily so the yoke does not settle to one side, thus spoiling it. For expediency sake, save old egg cartons to use when storing your preserved eggs with this method.

## Testing Eggs for Spoilage

No matter which method you choose to preserve eggs, always double check the condition of an egg before using it and throw out any cracked eggs you find. Over time, the egg whites will become a bit runny, but this will not affect the taste, nor is it harmful to eat.

A simple water test will help determine if eggs are good. Simply fill a pan with cold water. The eggs that float to the top must be discarded. The ones that settle to the bottom are safe to eat. As you crack open your preserved eggs, make sure to administer the "sniff test". If ever in doubt, toss them!

If you still aren't convinced about the safety of preserving eggs, powdered eggs can be purchased in number 10 cans at many food storage providers. You might also want to investigate egg-less cooking. Links for egg-less cooking have been provided at the end of this chapter.

## Additional Egg Preserving Methods

Victoria Ries generously contributed the following methods to preserve eggs:

Whether you are living "off-the-grid" or camping, fresh eggs must be kept cool to prevent spoilage. The ideal storage temperature for eggs is in the refrigerator at 40 degrees F. or 4 degrees C. Egg storage temperatures may be difficult to maintain when living off-the-grid or in primitive conditions, but not impossible. Even though powdered eggs are available for times when a refrigerator is not an option, nothing is as delicious as a couple of fresh eggs for breakfast.

Fresh egg storage lends itself to several methods; experiment with the ones that best suit you.

## Flour Sack Method

Purchase a large sack of flour and place fresh, unbroken eggs, points down, into the bottom of the flour sack. Cover these with a two-inch layer of flour and repeat the process until all your eggs are safely stored. The flour sack stays cool to cold when kept on a cement floor in the pantry or stored in a root cellar.

## Insulated Box Method

Line a large cardboard box with material such as polystyrene foam or foam packaging "peanuts" and nestle your fresh eggs, points down, in the foam. Place the box in a cool room under a bed; these conditions mimic a root cellar.

## The Cooler Method

Insulated coolers are ideal for storing fresh eggs and may be purchased inexpensively throughout the summer. Straw makes a good bed for your eggs. Begin by placing a thick wad of straw in the bottom of the cooler. Place your eggs, points down, into the straw, making sure there is a one-inch gap between them.

## Root Cellar Method

Store your eggs in straw inside apple boxes. Apple boxes have a foam inner liner that works well to keep each egg insulated and separate from the next. Simply place each egg in straw or sawdust and tuck them away on the cellar floor under the first shelf, stacking the boxes on top of each other.

## Stream or Spring Method

Storing eggs in running water was practiced in days of old before the invention of iceboxes or refrigerators. A simple wooden box was constructed with slats at the bottom and holes in the sides, in which to place waterproof foods such as butter or eggs. As the water from the stream or spring rushed through the box, it cooled the food, extending its "shelf-life".

## Preserving Butter

Butter is a staple that many of us would not want to be without. Sadly, butter is expensive, and getting more so by the day. Many of those who have been involved with preparedness for any length of time swear by home-canned butter (that is stored non-refrigerated), storing it for years in some cases, and consuming it with no ill effects. Here's the rub. For quite a while, canning and the consuming of non-refrigerated butter was all the rage with folks who were into preparedness. That all changed when someone decided to contact a government official at the FDA and was told home canned butter was dangerous to store because it could contain harmful bacteria. This red flag went viral, and soon, only the bravest (or the most stubborn) had not tossed out their carefully home canned butter. Personally, I suspect the same incorrect advice over storing un-refrigerated cheese came from the same playbook that advised against storing butter. But because I skipped pre-med chemistry, I should add a disclaimer that should you give canning butter a try, you do so at your own risk. Having said that, I haven't tossed out my canned butter, nor do I plan to.

## Preserving Cheese

For most of us, cheese is a staple, used in many of our favorite meals. As far the experts are concerned, cheese will not keep without refrigeration. That's an interesting statement when you consider that refrigeration wasn't invented until the 1940's and judging from old cook books, cheese was every bit the staple back then as it is today.

Information on preserving cheese without refrigeration was by far the most difficult search I had over the years. Finally, I discovered Kellene Bishop's blog site, and I would recommend it to anyone who wants information on preparedness who enjoys a delightful sense of humor (that would be Kellene!). Not only does she give thorough step-by-step instructions to preserve hard cheeses for years without refrigeration (the article is titled *Settling the Cheese Wax Controversy*), she does it with so much humor, it's a treat to learn! Her step-by-step instructions can be found at:

http://preparednesspro.wordpress.com/2009/08/19/settling-the-cheese-wax-controversy/

Kellene Bishop's main blog site, Preparedness Pro, is also worthwhile visiting: http://preparednesspro.com

# Sourdough Recipes

## Counter-Stored Sourdough Starter

### Ingredients

2 Cups All-Purpose Flour (can be white or wheat flour)*
2 Teaspoons Granulated Sugar*
1 Packet (2 ¼ teaspoons) Active Dry Yeast
2 Cups Warm Water (105 to 115 degrees F)*

* Whole wheat will not have the same rising properties and may take extra rising time. You can trade white for wheat flour if you chose.

* Adding sugar kick-starts your sourdough starter because yeast feeds on sugar, but you do not have to use it when dietary needs restrict sugar.

* Use distilled or bottled water if your water contains chlorine. Chlorine can stop the action of yeast.

### Instructions

Mix flour, sugar, and yeast together with a wooden spoon, never metal, in a sterile glass, glazed ceramic, or crockery pot with a 2 quart capacity. Again, NO plastic or metal.

Gradually stir in the warm water until the mixture becomes a thick paste.

Cover container with a dishcloth and allow to sit in a warm 70 to 80 degree room with no drafts. NOTE: temperatures over 100 degrees will kill the yeast.

The dishcloth allows wild yeast to pass into your starter (and why plastic wrap is not suggested). The mixture will bubble and foam as it ferments.

Stir once a day for 2 to 5 days. It is ready when it gives off a pleasant sour smell and is bubbly.

**Note**: to keep sourdough starter un-refrigerated, remove one cup of starter daily for use in baking or throw it away. Replace with one cup water and one cup flour and let sit out for several hours to re-activate before use in baking.

You can refrigerate your sourdough starter, covered, for as long as you want. Let it sit out overnight to reactivate the starter before baking. If left refrigerated for months, it may be necessary to restart the feeding process to "wake it up" so it will become active again. This may take 2 to 3 days.

**Another Sourdough Starter Recipe**

**Ingredients**

2 Cups Warm Water
1 Package Dry Yeast
2 Cups Flour
1 Tablespoon Sugar

Put warm water in crock. Sprinkle yeast over water and stir with a wooden spoon until dissolved. Add flour and sugar and mix until smooth. Cover and set aside 36 to 45 hours, stirring 3 to 4 times a day. Use 1 ½ cup starter for bread recipes.

May be kept refrigerated or counter-stored.

**And Yet Another Sourdough Starter Using Refrigerated Storage**

**Ingredients**

2 Cups Water
1 ½ Teaspoon Dry Yeast
2 Cups All-Purpose Flour
3 Tablespoons Sugar

Stir ingredients with a wooden spoon and cover with a clean dishtowel in a warm spot to catch wild yeast in the air. Stir once or twice a day until bubbles appear on the surface, which means wild yeast has been caught and fermentation has taken place.

Put into a snap-lid glass gar without actually snapping the lid and place in refrigerator. Bring to room temperature prior to using, which can be done by setting the jar out the night before you plan to use it.

Each time you use the sourdough starter, replace the amount you have used with equal parts flour and water. To adapt a regular recipe, add I cup sourdough starter, and use ½ cup less liquid and ½ cup less flour. Makes great cakes and full-textured breads.


**Everlasting Yeast Starter**

**Ingredients**

1 Quart Warm Potato Water *
½ Tablespoon Dry Yeast
1 Teaspoon Salt
2 Tablespoons Sugar
2 Cups White or Whole Wheat Flour

* To make warm potato water, grate one raw potato and place it in a bowl of water, covering the grated potato and letting it sit for several hours so that the starch from the potato can leach off into the bowl (you'll want approximately two cups of potato water). Remove the grated potato from the water. Add one tablespoon sugar to the starchy potato water and set aside to ferment. Within a few hours, you will see a foam form on the top of the potato water, which you will want to stir back into the potato water, but stir only once so that the fermenting can continue. Once the potato water has sat long enough to form a few inches of foam, scoop it off the top (foam only, not water), with a spoon, transferring it onto a piece of wax paper. Let dry. After skimming, continue to let the potato water ferment for approximately another 2 days for use in bread making. The dried, fermented foam can be stored in a tightly sealed container as yeast for later use.

**Warning**: If yeast foam from the potato water has a black, rust, or red colorization, do not use it to make dried yeast. This is an indication the yeast is bad and it will be necessary to make another batch.

Stir all ingredients together. Place mixture in a warm location to sit until ready for use in baking. Leave a small amount of Everlasting Yeast Starter for later use. Keep covered in a container in a cool location until a few hours before use.

Add the same ingredients above, except yeast, to the Everlasting Yeast Starter for future baking.

## * No-Yeast Breads *

### Irish Soda Bread

### Ingredients

3 Tablespoons Butter or Margarine (can be reconstituted)
2 ½ Cups All-Purpose Flour
2 Tablespoons Sugar
1 Teaspoon Baking Soda
1 Teaspoon Baking Powder
½ Teaspoon Salt
⅓ Cup Raisins (if desired)
¾ Cup Buttermilk

Heat oven to 375 degrees and prepare a greased cookie sheet.

Cut butter or butter-flavored shortening into flour, sugar, baking soda, baking powder, and salt in large bowl using a pastry blender, or crisscrossing with 2 knives until mixture resembles fine crumbs. Stir in raisins, if desired, and just enough buttermilk so dough leaves the side of the bowl.

Turn dough onto lightly floured surface and kneed 1 to 2 minutes or until smooth. Shape into round loaf, about 6 ½ inches in diameter. Place on greased cookie sheet. Cut an X shape about ½ inch deep through dough with floured knife.

Bake 35 to 45 minutes at 375 degrees.

## Buttermilk Substitute

The following can be used as a substitute for buttermilk—if you are without refrigeration, adjust proportions according to recipe amounts, as any remaining buttermilk substitute MUST be refrigerated.

### Ingredients

1 Cup Water
⅓ Cup Powdered Milk
1 Tablespoon Vinegar or Lemon

Let set in a warm place until thickened, usually 18 hours.

* Buttermilk (freeze-dried culture) can be purchased at grocery stores and will keep indefinitely.


## White Soda Bread

### Ingredients

4 Cups All-Purpose Flour
1 Teaspoon Baking Soda
1 Teaspoon Salt
14 Ounces Buttermilk or Buttermilk Substitute (see recipe above)

Preheat oven to 400 degrees.

In a large bowl combine all dry ingredients (can be sifted). Add buttermilk to form a sticky dough. Place on floured surface and knead lightly—but not too much, as it allows gas to escape. Shape into a round, flat bottomed shape in a greased and floured cake pan and cut a cross in the top of the dough.

Cover pan with another larger pan and bake for 30 minutes. Remove cover and cook for another 15 minutes to brown.

* The bottom of the bread will have a hollow sound when tapped when it is done.

\* Cover bread with a tea towel and sprinkle water over the cloth to keep bread moist.

## Spoon Bread

### Instructions

Place 3 cups self-rising flour in a large mixing bowl. Make a depression in the middle of the flour. Add a lump of shortening, about the size of a black walnut. Pour buttermilk, or buttermilk substitute (see above), in the depression and begin stirring the flour closest to the center, working out to the sides of the bowl. If the batter looks too dry, add a little more buttermilk. Batter should be sticky, but not liquid.

There are several options when baking spoon bread: you can grease and heat a cast iron skillet and cook it on top of the stove, or it can be baked in a fireplace on top of hot coals, or you can bake it in a 400 degree oven. Depending on your cooking method, your spoon bread should be done in approximately 15 to 20 minutes. The moister the batter, the higher and lighter your bread will be. However, the moister the batter, the longer it will take to bake.

\* To make the bread appear smoother, you can wet the top with a little water and smooth the batter with the back of a spoon.

\* Spoon Bread makes great 'soppers' to dip into gravy, soups, bean dishes, or whatever else you cook that could use a bit of warm bread.

## Quick Bread

### Ingredients

1 ½ Cups Milk
6 Teaspoons Baking Powder
1 Teaspoon Salt
½ Teaspoon Sugar
1 Tablespoon Melted Shortening

Mix flour, salt, sugar, baking powder, and melted shortening thoroughly. Slowly add milk (or reconstituted powdered milk, or a combination of 1 ¼ cups canned milk and 1 ¼ cups water)—enough to make a stiff dough. Bake in a greased bread pan at 350 degrees for 55 minutes.

## Baking Powder Biscuits

### Ingredients

5 Cups Flour
6 Heaping Teaspoons Baking Powder
1 Teaspoon Salt
4 Teaspoons Sugar
1 ½ Cups Shortening
2 Cups Milk (or reconstituted powdered milk or 1 cup canned milk and 1 cup water)

Sift dry ingredients. Blend in shortening with pastry blender. Pour in milk and mix well until dough is formed into a ball. Roll out on a floured board to ½ inch thickness. Cut into rounds. Bake at 450 degrees for 20 minutes or until golden brown. Makes 30 biscuits.

## Activities for Children: You're Gonna Need 'Em!

It's likely a crisis won't register with the children in your group. If only it were so for the adults! Keeping them busy will do wonders for the sanity of the adults in your group. The following are finger paint and Play Dough recipes that can be made with ingredients you have in your pantry.

## Recipe for Homemade Finger Paint

### Ingredients

½ Cup Cornstarch
3 Tablespoons Sugar
½ Teaspoon Salt
2 Cups Cold Water

### Directions

Mix above ingredients together in a saucepan. Cook on low heat 10 to 15 minutes, stirring until smooth and the mixture thickens. Let it cool.

Divide the cooled finger paint into separate bowls and add the desired food coloring. Store finger paints in containers with lids or ziplock bags so they will not dry out.


## Recipe for Homemade Play Dough

### Ingredients

1 Cup Cornstarch
2 Cups Baking Soda
1 ½ Cups Water

### Directions

Stir above ingredients until smooth and cook over medium heat until thick. Place on a plate or bowl and covered until cooled. Add desired food coloring into the cooled Play Dough and kneed until coloring is mixed throughout. Store it in containers with tight lids or ziplock bags to keep it from drying out.

# List of Suggested Suppliers and Reading Material

**Note:** Although the author has studied, and in some cases ordered from the following suggested sites, it is always wise to do your own research for the best pricing and availability for your geographic location. At the time of the publication of *Survival: Prepare Before Disaster Strikes,* each site listed was operational.

## Water Glass Supplier

http://www.lehmans.com

## Eggless Cooking Recipes

http://www.egglesscooking.com/

http://eggless.com/

http://www.your-vegetarian-kitchen.com/eggless-desserts.html

http://allrecipes.com/Recipe/eggless-pasta/detail.aspx

## A Great Article in Defense of Home-Canning Butter

http://www.preparednesspro.com/blog/catching-up-with-the-truth-about-expiration-dates-and-butter/#more-6032

## Home-Canning Butter Instructions

http://www.preparednesspro.com/blog/to-bottle-or-not-to-bottle-butter/

## Dutch Oven & Camp-Style Recipes

http://boyslife.org/outdoors/outdoorarticles/12765/great-reflector-oven-recipes/

*What's Cooking America—Lots of Cast Iron Recipes*
http://whatscookingamerica.net/CastIronRecipes.htm

## Recipes for Meals, Baked Goods, Desserts

*100's of Dutch Oven Recipes*
http://www.recipesfromscratch.com/dutch/index.htm

*The Net Woods Virtual Campsites*
http://www.netwoods.com/d-cooking.html

## Solar Cooking Recipes

*Solar Oven Society Recipes*
http://www.solarovens.org/recipes/

## Food Storage Recipes

http://everydayfoodstorage.net/food-storage-recipes

http://beprepared.com/recipes

http://foodstoragemadeeasy.net/self-reliance/cooking-from-scratch/

http://www.providentliving.org/content/list/0,11664,2017-1,00.html

http://www.mormonchic.com/recipe/

http://dealstomeals.com/docs/FOOD_STORAGE_RECIPES.pdf

http://www.scribd.com/doc/2229985/Food-Storage-Recipes

http://dinnerisinthejar.com/

http://peaceofpreparedness.com/Resource%20Library/Recipies/1-month_kit_RECIPES.pdf

# Chapter 18

# When Things Go Bump in the Night

*"I know God will not give me anything I can't handle.
I just wish that He didn't trust me so much."*
Mother Teresa

Most of us would agree the best way to stay safe during a time of unrest is to remain as small a target as possible. If an economic meltdown or a weather-related crisis disrupts life as we know it, there will be looters and worse who'd be more than willing to take what they need by theft or by force.

If you have based your assumptions of survivability on the way folks made it through the Great Depression, you may want to rethink your plan.

## People Lived Differently During the Great Depression

Let's examine why. In the 1930's most folks were either debt free or close to it. It was the norm back then to put 50% down on a home, and many paid for them outright. The average home was relatively small and bedrooms were tiny in comparison with today's standards. Closets were even tinier because it was not the norm in those days to have more than a few dresses, slacks and shirts. Furnishings were saved for and purchased one at a time as money allowed and were normally utilitarian.

Back then, it was not unusual for several generations to have been born and raised and died in the same small community. Family members were there for one another whenever the need arose. In those days, folks tucked money aside in a cookie jar for a rainy day. They grew gardens, and most lived near farms, where they could purchase fruits and vegetables affordably. Many kept chickens for their eggs and meat. To "put aside" any overflow from the garden, folk's home canned. They saved up for the family automobile and took care of it, many times doing routine maintenance themselves, and they nursed these automobiles until they basically fell apart. Many still used woodstoves for heat and bathroom facilities and knob and tube electricity was a relatively new invention. Their "lifeline" was not the telephone, because they all had party lines where telephone operators could listen to conversations—whom could be counted on for salacious gossip. They knew how to entertain themselves, for the radio was their one vice and children didn't need a "family room" to hold all their toys.

Most important when comparing today's world with what life was like in the years leading up to the Great Depression was that people did not expect the government to shelter and feed them. They were on their own, and they did quite nicely, thank you.

## The Era of Instant Gratification & Entitlement

Now compare that with today. The average household is $18,000 in debt, with the lion's share being credit card debt that if paid off with minimum monthly payments can easily take 30 years to pay off. Many of those who have managed to hang on to their homes are financially upside down in them, owing much more on their mortgages than what they are able to sell them for. Nowadays homes have walk-in closets the size of the average bedroom found in a 1930's bungalow. We now require "family rooms" to house huge flat screen TV's and electronics and we buy our children so many toys they couldn't possibly fit in their oversized closets. With the advent of travel, families no longer remain in the same communities where they were raised and the family unity of the generations is no longer seen as necessary or even desirable. Today, most families do not have extra cash to tuck away in a cookie jar we may or may not possess. Most couples have at least two cars that are traded in routinely, and this does not address the cars purchased—on credit—for our children. Few of us live anywhere near a farm where we can buy fruits and vegetables and most do not grow gardens, or raise chickens, and forget about home canning! Except for more rural locations, the average American depends upon the electrical grid and the gas company to heat our homes and to be able to cook. Should electricity or the water supply suddenly get knocked off-grid, few of us would have a clue about how to survive without these conveniences.

The U.S. population has never experienced a complete disconnect from normal everyday life. The closest we have come was the Great Depression. The problem with the assumption that "we've been there, done that, and survived" is that it's a misnomer. We *weren't* there, did *not* do that, and *have not* survived to the other side with a populace that expects the government to feed and shelter them. That mindset and the current expectation of instant gratification and entitlement is a fairly new phenomenon. We haven't had reason to test it and I pray we never do.

Should life disintegrate to the point that food supplies are disrupted, and utilities and services are no longer available, when transportation and communications fall apart, we are all in for a very difficult time.

Preparedness will go a long way towards survival. If you have planned ahead for alternative heat, cooking, and toilet facilities, your life will be a Shangri-La compared to folks who assumed they would get bailed out in their time of need. If you've put aside food storage, have prepared for gardening and home canning, and have put aside medical supplies and hygiene necessities, yours and the lives of your loved ones will be survivable.

## Now All You Need to Do is to Protect It!

It is possible that communities and neighborhoods will come together to help one another during a crisis. We have all seen inspirational selflessness on the evening news during times of crisis like 9-11,

Katrina, and when a hurricane or tornado rips the safety out from under those caught unaware. Even in the midst of total collapse, many will be drawn to help one another. The question we should all be asking ourselves is will this last during a protracted crisis? Will goodwill continue to flow to communities and neighborhoods if there comes a time when food supplies and services are no longer available?

At such a time, it's likely even the most caring of folks may be driven to acts they would have never thought themselves capable of. To watch loved ones go hungry can slant the perspective of even the best of us.

Eventually, if things were to continue to degrade, making yourself as small a target as possible will have new meaning, for it won't just be about keeping your preparedness to yourself, it will mean camouflaging it from infiltrators and looters.

At a time when society has broken down, there will be bands of looters and worse on the move. They will be looking for signs that your location and your preparedness goods are worth attacking.

## Let's Examine That Further

At a time when the grid goes down and electricity has become a distant memory, lighting an oil lamp to read by with the curtains drawn would be unwise. Why? It's simple. You have just sent the bad guy an engraved invitation to help himself to whatever you have! Only someone with supplies will have the means to provide light in a grid-down situation. For this reason, you should have black plastic sheeting or black garbage bags and tape set aside to block out telltale light coming from your home. This is doubly important for those who live in an urban setting. Looters and roving gangs won't have far to go to find their targets in a dense population. Just make sure you're one step ahead of them.

Opportunists will also be on the lookout for the sound of a generator during a grid-down situation. Think about times you've been camping or gone for a hike in the woods. The peacefulness was incredible, wasn't it? Now consider that quiet blanketing whole communities. The sound of a generator may be music to your ears, and it will offer the convenience to run lights, appliances and, if large enough, a refrigerator, TV, or any number of appliances. However, this convenience should always be tempered with weighing the risks of telegraphing your preparedness over great distances, leading looters right to your door.

Looters and bands of opportunists will also be listening for the sound of ATV's, snowmobiles, and chainsaws. Think carefully before you run these items if your area has drawn unsavory elements.

Other telltale signs the opportunist will be on the lookout for is firewood, tools, gasoline barrels, water containment barrels and ATV's sitting in plain sight on your property. Each of these items will be in great demand during a time of prolonged crisis. So don't make it easy for the bad guys! Keep everything out of sight as much as humanly possible.

## Communications

If you have already planned ahead for communication needs with a ham radio or two-way radios, know that their signal can be intercepted, and your location discovered. For this reason, those who have studied this inherent flaw suggest keeping communications short and when possible, plan to transmit away from your immediate location. Never announce your location or identify yourself during emergency communications.

## Fencing and Watch Dogs

There are certain things we won't be able to hide. A garden is a good example. Gardens are long-term answers for a reliable, ongoing food supply and anyone interested in basic survival will have put aside heirloom seed and will, by necessity, grow gardens. Chickens and other farm animals are other invitations to a looter or a roving gang. Solar panels are another item the bad guys will be checking for.

If your property is not fenced, you should think about putting one up. It should be built solid with no gaps and as tall as the codes in your area allow. This won't stop someone from hopping your fence (unless you add razor wire), but with the addition of a large dog with attitude in the quotient, I doubt your place will be as attractive as it otherwise would have been.

When I lived in Alaska before moving to North Idaho, my neighbors posted signs on their eight-foot cyclone fence that read: **My Rottweiler Can Make This Fence In 8 Seconds Flat. Can You?** I laughed every time I passed that sign, but I doubt if a looter would have.

A large dog is a great safety measure for a time of mayhem. They will alert you to trouble well before you are able to hear the sound of an intruder approaching your home. They are loyal, and even the most kind-hearted of pooches will defend their "pack"—meaning you and your group. They can also protect your garden and chickens from four-legged creatures as well. If you decide to keep a dog for protection, be sure to set aside enough food and medical supplies for an extended period of time.

If for some reason you can't keep a dog, you can create the illusion that you do. An extra heavy dog chain wrapped around a porch post with a worn, heavy collar (maybe black with metal studs) trailing in the yard will give a looter nightmares over its possible owner and they will likely keep going. It doesn't hurt to add a chewed-up dog bowl, either. If you *really* want to go the extra mile, do what a friend who's known for his practical jokes suggested: add a half chewed deer leg next to the bowl.

## Beef Up Your Doors & Avoid Home Invasions

It is important to make your home as impenetrable as possible to a would-be intruder. If you have flimsy doors, it's time to switch them out. A solid metal door without a window that can be easily smashed in by a gloved first is a good start. Yes, there will be less light warming the interior of your home, but it's far better to deal with a little inconvenience than to endanger the safety of your loved ones.

Doorjambs should be sturdy. There are doorjambs on the market today that have been tested to withstand even a battering ram (links provided at the end of this chapter). Be sure you use reinforced, heavy-duty hinges as well.

Home invasions many times involve the attacker kicking in the door to gain entrance into your home. Good thing you took care of the door issue, isn't it?

According to police reports, many times the homeowner themselves were the weak link in home invasions. How? They opened the door to a "deliveryman", or "repair man" or someone requesting help…they lost their dog…or their cat…or their girlfriend. A peephole is a good investment that will allow you to see who is on the other side of the door before inviting in your worst nightmare. For this reason, you should never allow a child to answer the door. They do not have the necessary discernment to judge whether or not a stranger can be trusted.

Never pinch pennies when it comes to safety. This includes depending on a safety chain as your only line of defense. They never work. All it takes is a swift kick by a determined assailant, and they're indoors and threatening you and your loved ones.

## Seek Expert Advice

There are entire books written about home safety and weaponry. When searching for expert advice, it is advisable to look for information centered on long-term survival. There is a big difference between defending yourself against a random home invasion and preparing for an onslaught of looters and gangs for an undetermined length of time.

I suggest you research online survival and preparedness sites for advice on the best books on the subject and to search for recommended classes that specialize in tactical and self-defense training. There is nothing like actual experience to gain the mindset of a survivor.

## Plan for the Worst Case Scenario

If your location is visited by a determined horde, or a handful of panicked looters, and your safety contingent consists of you and your spouse, you'll need back up. Do you have neighbors you could depend on? If so, you don't necessarily have to hand them a laundry list of the preparedness goods you've put aside, but you might want to discuss a "what if" scenario with them; one that might include 2-way radios, where you could send for help, and they likewise. Or you can go one step further and coordinate a "call tree" involving your neighborhood, where you will all have each other's backs.

This is the reason why many veteran "preppers" have chosen to ban together with other like-minded folks. If you do decide to band together, the next step will be to discuss, as a group, where the line in the sand will be set. Will you use force if a looter shows up to steal supplies or does that line in the sand stand only when confronted by force? The emotional make-up of a group goes a long ways towards what measures are followed. But these determinations must be made *before* the looter comes for a visit; otherwise you'll waste valuable time. Hesitation can cost lives!

## Find a Safe Place

If there are children in the group and there's trouble, you should have an agreed upon plan for their safety. Who is assigned to care for them? Where is the safest place to duck and hide until the coast is clear? Planning for such things and acting upon them quickly will offer the best outcome for unexpected emergencies.

## Store Food and Water Indoors

Hopefully, you made plans to store at least two weeks worth of food and water indoors, for it isn't only necessary during a nuclear event. It is just as likely you will need it if you're forced to wait out a band of looters. Don't fool yourself into believing there will never come a time that you can't go out to a food storage shed or draw water from the well.

## Bugging Out

Leaving a location when it has become unsafe was touched upon in Chapter 2, *Are You Ready?* You may hear this called "bugging out" (ergo a bug-out kit). Fleeing a location and leaving behind valuable provisions is never an optimal situation, but it may be necessary.

Plan to stash provisions outside your immediate location, where they can be retrieved out of sight of the bad guys. This requires placing survival goods in watertight buckets and burying them well before an unsafe situation presents itself. When in doubt, encase the buckets in heavy plastic bags for safekeeping. Most preppers stash food, medical supplies, hunting and fishing gear, as well as camp gear. It will be important to have a water purifier, compass, bullets, matches and topographical map of your area. Many of these items will already be packed away in your emergency kit (never unpack them as they are your lifeline). You will want to scout out an area, before an emergency, that has a water source and is as safe as possible.

Your destination might not involve fleeing, however. If the situation is so out of control that you're forced to relocate, that same situation will exist for your neighbors. If plans have been made before the fact for a neighborhood to join forces when things get out of control, there's a much higher likelihood of survival.

# List of Suggested Suppliers and Reading Material

**Note:** Although the author has studied, and in some cases ordered from the following suggested sites, it is always wise to do your own research for the best pricing and availability for your geographic location. At the time of the publication of *Survival: Prepare Before Disaster Strikes,* each site listed was operational.

## Reinforced Door Parts & Jams

http://www.armorconcepts.com/

*How to Avoid a Home Invasion and Other Safety Issues*
http://www.crimedoctor.com/homeinvasion.htm

## Survival/Preparedness Blog

*Thousands of survival-related articles, including tactical, surveillance, and more*
http://www.survivalblog.com/

## Top 10 Guard Dogs

http://www.petmedsonline.org/top-10-best-guard-dog-breeds.html

# Chapter 19

# Bartering for Goods & Services

*"All government—indeed, every human benefit and enjoyment, every virtue and every prudent act—is founded on compromise and barter."*
Edmund Burk

We could bury our face in how-to books from dawn to dusk every day of our lives and never know everything we need to know for long-term survival. Think over the past few years, when things came up unexpectedly and you ended up on the phone, scheduling a repairman to come over, or you made that unexpected trip to the hardware store for that thing-a-ma-gig that went with the watch-a-ma-call-it. If we had the space to store everything we needed, and the money to buy it, and the intuition to look years into the future and know what would go wrong so we could study up and learn the basics, we'd have all the bases covered. But this is the real world, and we have to do the very best that we can and expect some slips along the way.

At some point, we're going to need help. In the event of a long-term crisis, we may need a glazier to replace a broken window; or we may need more home canning lids; or someone to weld a broken part that is no longer available. And that's just for those of us who are prepared.

There are two approaches to bartering that will, by necessity, be used during a crisis that lasts any length of time: services (ability and training), or goods (everything else).

We'll start with the "everything else" category.

Even when retailers are able to keep their doors open in the midst of a crisis, it is possible that truckers may be stuck in gridlock and basic supplies may be difficult or impossible to find. Having a few of the items that are listed below for barter to exchange for goods and services will be like manna from heaven.

Many of us are *already* struggling to put aside preparedness goods and food storage for our own personal needs. The good news is that a bartering cache can start with inexpensive items purchased in quantity. The recommended items found under the first list below, $1.00 Store Bartering Goods, can be found at both Dollar Stores and on sale at grocery outlet stores. In fact, having less expensive canned goods available for barter may be in your favor, for many people will not have arranged for alternative cooking.

If you have a bit more cash flow to invest in bartering goods, there are many mid-priced items that will be sought after that will offer bartering possibilities. You will notice books are listed here. In the midst of an ongoing crisis, people will need information on gardening, first aid, books on home repairs, survival manuals and the like.

For those of you with the cash flow, the high-ticket items listed will be in great demand in a crisis. However, you will want to weigh the safety issues of having valuable, in-demand goods against the risk of theft or looting.

Just as with personal preparedness, it is never a good idea to share what you have put aside for bartering with anyone outside those you know you can trust.

Specific geographic locations will have unique preparedness needs. Some of the items listed below are universal needs, while others are not. If you want further ideas for bartering items, please refer to Chapter 11, *Survival Goods*. The items below have been selected because they will be the most in demand in a full-blown crisis and, accordingly, they will be the first things to fly off the shelves.

# $1.00 Store Bartering Goods

<u>Basic Survival Goods</u>: Candles, lighter fluid, wood matches, twine, wire

<u>Canned Food</u>: Beans, chili, fruit, vegetables, soup, stew

<u>Cleaning Products</u>: Bleach, kitchen pot-scrubbers, liquid laundry soap, liquid dish soap, scrubbing powder

<u>Gardening</u>: Gardening gloves

<u>Health & First Aid</u>: Magnified reading glasses (assorted strengths), bandages, rubbing alcohol, tweezers, Vaseline

<u>Hygiene</u>: Body lotion, body soap, dental floss, toothpaste, nail clippers, razors, shampoo, sunburn lotion, toothbrushes, toothpaste

<u>Kitchen Supplies</u>: Can openers, hot pads, plastic containers with lids, plastic wrap, pot-scrubbers, wooden matches, tin foil, zip-lock bags

<u>Spices & Baking Basics</u>: Baking powder, baking soda, garlic powder, pepper, salt

# Pricier Bartering Goods

<u>Basic Survival Goods</u>: Charcoal, food storage buckets, gasoline containers, honing oil (for axe sharpening), lamps (oil & kerosene), lamp replacement wicks and chimneys, lighter fluid, nylon cord, propane cylinders, propane heater heads, water containers

<u>Basic Tools & Supplies</u>: Allen wrenches, bolts (assorted), box cutters, hammers, nails (assorted), nuts (assorted), pliers, screwdrivers, washers (assorted), wood saws, wrenches, wood glue

<u>Books</u>: Boy Scout manual, edible wild plant manuals, first aid manuals, home canning, home-storage cookbooks, gardening, holistic medicine, meat curing, seed saving

<u>Building Materials</u>: Heavy-mill plastic, lumber, 2 X 4's, plywood, roofing material, caulking, drywall mud, drywall tape, tarps, stakes

<u>Camp Gear</u>: Backpacks, camp stoves, camp stove fuel, coolers, compass, duffle bags, lantern mantles, portable camp toilets, sleeping bags, tents

<u>Clothing</u>: Cotton kerchiefs, ear muffs, gloves, hiking boots, rain jackets, rubber boots, socks, warm clothing, warm hats, warm jackets, tennis shoes, work boots, underwear

<u>Entertainment</u>: Board games, cards, coloring crayons, colored pencils, colored markers, coloring books, construction paper, craft glue, dice, journals, pencils, pens, writing paper

<u>Food</u>: Assorted spices (see Chapter 10, *Layering Food Storage*), baby formula, beans (dry), brown sugar, bullion, coffee, cooking oil, dog food, drinks (powdered), honey, hot cocoa, milk (powdered and evaporated), pancake mix, peanut butter, popcorn, rice, soup base (powdered), syrup, tea, tuna fish, vinegar, wheat, white flour, white sugar, yeast

<u>Gardening</u>: Rakes, shovels, spades, trowels

<u>Health & First Aid</u>: Baby diaper ointment, burn ointment, eye wash, first aid kits, gauze bandaging, mosquito repellant, Neosporin (or other antibiotic ointments), over-the-counter medications (refer to Chapter 11, *Survival Goods*), vitamins

<u>Household</u>: Ant traps, batteries (all types), blankets, carbon monoxide alarm, garbage bags, garbage cans, clothesline, clothes pegs, duct tape, fire alarms, fire extinguishers, flashlights, hand pumps, lantern hangers, laundry washboard, mop, mop bucket, mouse traps, pillows, roach poison, scissors, sewing thread and needles, siphons, sleeping mats, window insulation

<u>Hygiene</u>: Antibacterial soap, baby wipes, diapers (cloth), diaper pins, rubber pants, feminine pads, shaving cream, toilet paper

<u>Kitchen & Cooking</u>: canning supplies, knife sharpening file, manual wheat grinder (basic), paper plates, paraffin wax, plastic cups, plastic utensils

<u>Safety</u>: Pepper spray, stun gun, hornet spray (used for self-defense)

# High-End Bartering Goods

<u>Animals</u>: Chickens, goats

<u>Basic Survival</u>: Firewood (seasoned), generator (diesel/gas/solar), propane cook stove, water purifier and replacement filters, wood cook stove, wood heat stove, sleeping bags, tents

<u>Fuel</u>: Diesel, gasoline, 55-gallon steel barrels

<u>Gardening</u>: Garden fencing (deer-proof, 8-foot T-fence and wire), heirloom garden seed

<u>Kitchen Implements</u>: Cast iron cookware, fire-pit tripods, manual wheat grinder (Country Living Wheat Mill), reflector ovens, solar cookers

<u>Safety & Hunting</u>: Ammunition, fishing rods and supplies, guns, hunting bow and arrows, hunting knives

<u>Transportation</u>: Bicycles, bicycle tires and pumps and patch kits, carts, wagons

<u>Tree-Felling/Wood Gathering</u>: Axes, chainsaws, hatchets, splitting mauls, two-man saws, wedges

# Bartering Know-How

Some of the services that will be in demand during a long-term meltdown may require training. The effort will be worth it. When you contemplate a day when services may be unavailable at any cost, there will be many in-demand skills people will be eager to barter for. If the neighbor lady down the street has a leak in her roof, for instance, and you happen to be a roofer or have carpentry skills, she'd probably be happy to barter your expertise for something she has…possibly those chickens you never got around to buying.

Welding will be in huge demand. Just think of the repairs that will be needed when parts are no longer available! Car repair is another skill that will be valuable. Each field of expertise comes with the tools of the trade. If it's welding that interests you, then setting yourself up with a generator for a power-driven welder, or a propane-run welder will greatly increase your bartering capabilities.

If you know next to nothing about food preparation and the lady down the street just happens to be an excellent cook she'd probably be happy to trade her cooking expertise for a portion of the venison you hunted.

If your expertise happens to be sewing, an antique trundle machine that isn't dependent upon electricity will offer plenty of bartering power. The same goes for taking in laundry. All you will need is a clothesline, clothes pegs, tubs, an old-fashioned laundry board and a wringer, which can come from a wringer mop bucket.

Clearly, bartering does not always require training. If you built the smoke house you've been mulling over, you could trade smoking the neighbor's game in exchange for something you need.

The simplest way to get a feel for what skills are likely to be barter friendly during a long-term crisis can be figured out by sitting down and watching a few westerns. You'll notice people used firewood to heat their homes and to cook. Repairs were done with manual tools. They hunted and fished and some shod horses while others cared for farm animals. Others built fences, were midwives, were dentists and doctors, dug wells, sold garden fruits and vegetables, they babysat, they cleaned houses and they took in borders.

Although it's imperative to put aside preparedness goods to survive, if a crisis is of long duration, eventually these items will run out and we will have to turn to our skills, knowledge, and sweat-equity to survive. Just as important as preparedness goods are to survival, so is a mindset of self-sufficiency and a can-do attitude. There won't be any wusses walking out the other side intact. I'm not talking about physical strength, although being as fit as possible can't hurt. It's more of a belief in yourself, that no matter what…you and your loved ones will survive.

If *Survival: Prepare Before Disaster Strikes* is the first book you have read on preparedness, please be sure it isn't your last. There are many subjects surrounding survival, each one a book of its own. Read as many books and manuals on the subject of survival as possible. Books on gardening and edible wild foods specific to your climate zone, first aid, and animal husbandry should be purchased for easy reference that can be found at used bookstores if need be. Take whatever courses you feel you will need: first aid, self-defense, fitness and then move on to the next hurdle. No one said it was easy—it isn't! But you'll be a better person for having extended yourself.

I encourage everyone who lives in a congested, urban location to consider having a back-up location where there will be plentiful water, and where you are more likely to be left in peace.

I would like to close this book in the spirit of giving. Each person who is able and willing to help another, and does so freely, will be greatly blessed.

# List of Suggested Suppliers and Reading Material

**Note:** Although the author has studied, and in some cases ordered from the following suggested sites, it is always wise to do your own research for the best pricing and availability for your geographic location. At the time of the publication of *Survival: Prepare Before Disaster Strikes*, each site listed was operational.

## More on Bartering

*Detailed List of In-demand Barter Goods*
http://www.survival-homestead.com/barter-goods.html

*Good Advice on Bartering Smartly*
http://www.surviveabide.com/Advanced/Financial/Financial%20-%20Bartering%20Skill.htm

# About the Author

*Barbara Fix* was born and raised on an Alaskan homestead, dodging moose on the way to the outhouse and playing Scrabble by lamplight. She currently lives off-grid in North Idaho with fewer moose and alternative power. Barbara is a published author of numerous articles and advice columns related to preparedness and gardening.